PRAISE FOR

This book is a "gift fro_____ _____ so clearly and plainly articulates the spiritual and universal laws that govern our existence. It certainly changed my life...and more importantly, the way I see my entire existence. It is life-altering material presented in the most easily understood language I have ever encountered. Though I was deeply hurt by the pain and tragedy of the terrorist attacks (9/11/01), I spent the day thinking about the laws and how they work. I applied them and came up with different ways of acting, thinking, and releasing to give myself (and others) back the power that was intended to be removed by the fear and terror that were inflicted upon us all. I recommend the book to all of my clients and am now selling them at my office and workshops.
... Gigi Moser, Certified Medical Hypnotherapist (9/13/01)

Vibrational Harmony is "the book" that makes the whole concept of Universal Law come to life and make sense. Not only does one understand why most programming and motivational seminars don't work in the long run, Beverly gives you the action steps to release negativity and install new programming to fit your own needs!
... Dr. Skip Skibsted, DC, DICS

For the first time in my life, the major missing pieces of the puzzle in self-happiness and creating a wonderful life have fallen into place. After having gotten the "ah ha" of what Beverly Nadler teaches, I put her Energy Model of life to work for me. My money-consciousness has suddenly gone from lack to abundance literally overnight. Other life-validating events are occurring also. This is proof enough for me that this brilliant lady has given me THE keys to unlocking my life.
...Diana Huston, Retail Business Owner

Beverly Nadler's knowledge, understanding and presentation of the way life really works (the natural laws of the universe) has already changed the lives of literally thousands. With her new book,"Vibratonal Harmony", she has the opportunity to help millions more.
...Dr. W. Karl Parker, President, Karl Parker Seminars

The book challenges us to embark on a glowing future, filled with unlimited potential in all aspects of our lives. Beverly walks us through simple steps towards maximizing and fulfilling our personal desires by removing limitations, focusing on our goals, attracting what is needed and reaping our rewards.
…Owen "Lynn", Stitz, President and Lucille Whiting Stitz, Vice President, Midwest Research of Michigan, Inc.

A very good job of taking deep, philosophical subjects and translating them into useful tools for living a better life. I'm pleased her work acknowledges and reflects her study and application of several principles developed by my late father.
…George T. Fleet, Jr., President, Concept-Therapy Institute

Beverly is a clear and eloquent teacher. I have seen her work inspire and touch many people. Her new book is original in its presentation and her techniques are easy to use and very profound for their simplicity.
…Reverend Linda Bardes, Founder and Director, New Haven Religious Science Center for Dynamic Living

Beverly's new work takes a bold step forward, empowering us to work in harmony with the energy all around us. With Beverly's help we can put aside our fear, mistrust and insecurities, and achieve our personal and business goals by learning that energy can be instantly re-directed and transformed. Thank you!
…Joseph Mackey, President, MiracleNet.com

After having read and practiced just about every healing modality (from leading authors to Zen Buddhism, psychotherapy and prescription medicine), I finally discovered powerful and effective practices for healing my life. Now others can experience this enormous transformation and discovery in her wonderful book.
…Joan Patrice Klein, Interior Designer, Feng Shui Consultant

Beverly Nadler has a unique way of uncovering Universal Truths and empowering her readers and listeners alike to take charge of their destiny. Her dynamic presentations and writings can serve as a beacon, lighting our way to the mastery of life.
…Dr. Shoshana Margolin, Naturopath, Homeopath, Author, Developer of Quantum Therapy

VIBRATIONAL HARMONY

**Why We Don't Get What We Want
And How We Can**

BEVERLY NADLER

Vibrational Harmony: Why We Don't Get What We Want And How We Can
© Copyright 2001 Beverly Nadler. All rights reserved.
(Originally copyrighted as: *Good Vibrations* in 2000)

No part of this work may be reproduced or transmitted in any form or by any means, electronic or mechanical, including photocopying and recording, or by any information storage or retrieval system, except as may be expressly permitted by the Copyright Act or in writing by permission from the author.

Disclaimer: Nothing in this book should be construed as a promise of benefits or a guarantee of results to be achieved. The author disclaims any liability directly or indirectly as a result of the use or application of any of the contents of this book. The processes, techniques and recommendations in this book are not meant for diagnosis or treatment and do not replace competent professional health care.

Unlimited Visions
911 East Main Street (Suite 249)
Stamford, Connecticut 06902
203-973-0130

Cover Design: Linda Kosarin
Kosarin Information Design
New York, NY

Printed in Victoria, Canada

```
National Library of Canada
Cataloguing in Publication Data

Nadler, Beverly.
   Vibrational harmony
   ISBN 1-55212-854-7
   1. Self-realization.   2. Success.   I. Title.
BF637.S4N318 2001          158'.1         C2001-911059-6
```

TRAFFORD

This book was published *on-demand* **in cooperation with Trafford Publishing.**
On-demand publishing is a unique process and service of making a book available for retail sale to the public taking advantage of on-demand manufacturing and Internet marketing.
On-demand publishing includes promotions, retail sales, manufacturing, order fulfilment, accounting and collecting royalties on behalf of the author.

Suite 6E, 2333 Government St., Victoria, B.C. V8T 4P4, CANADA
Phone	250-383-6864	Toll-free	1-888-232-4444 (Canada & US)
Fax	250-383-6804	E-mail	sales@trafford.com
Web site	www.trafford.com	TRAFFORD PUBLISHING IS A DIVISION OF TRAFFORD HOLDINGS LTD.	
Trafford Catalogue #01-0254	www.trafford.com/robots/01-0254.html		

10   9   8   7   6   5   4

ACKNOWLEDGEMENTS

I would like to acknowledge and give thanks to the many people who helped make this book possible:

To my parents who are no longer with me -- I thank them for the insatiable hunger they gave me, to search, to know and to understand.

To my lovely daughters who make me proud to be their mom:

> Karen, with her brilliant mind, whose parenting skills and ability to turn a house into a loving home is a rare gift.
>
> Lauren, whose superb talent as an actor, director and coach and her commitment to her craft fills me with awe.
>
> Denise, whose stunning voice, teaching skills and ability to create music and lyrics that heal never cease to amaze me.

To my granddaughter, Jackie, a beautiful and very special young lady who is wise beyond her years.

To my brothers, Norman and Gary, and my Aunt Betty with whom I've spent delightful hours discussing spiritual and philosophical principles.

To my friend and colleague, Joyce Barrie, whose support, keen sense of humor and creative problem-solving skills add much needed levity and laughter to my life.

To Diana Huston, whose evolutionary path and journey parallels my own, and whose valuable insights and input help me refine and define my teaching.

To Rev. Linda Bardes, whose friendship and inspired Science of Mind treatments do so much to nourish my spirit and soul.

To Linda Kosarin, who designed a beautiful cover that perfectly depicts what I want to express.

To my all my dear friends whose relationships I treasure -- for being part of my life and for encouraging me to believe in myself and my work.

To my accompanist and coach, Jerry King, who helps me balance the intensity of teaching with the joy of singing.

To my many students, newsletter subscribers and clients for allowing me to participate in their lives, share what I know…and learn from them.

To the late chiropractic icon Dr. James W Parker, on whose platforms I developed many of my programs, and his son, Dr. W Karl Parker, who continues to carry the torch.

To the late Dr. Thurman Fleet and the Concept-Therapy Institute whose teachings of truth inspired and motivated me to discover my mission.

To the chiropractors and healers who helped me when I was critically ill in body, mind and spirit.

To Dr. Rob Parker, whose insightful and intuitive healing session led to the inspiration that became this book.

To Eve Kerwin, whose unique spiritual healing work leads me to greater clarity in my own mission.

To the many teachers, motivators and authors whose work touched and inspired me on my evolutionary path.

To my colleagues and peers for the insights I gain from our lively and enlightening exchanges.

I gratefully acknowledge the contributions of the following Energy Psychology professionals.

>   Dr. Shoshana Margolin for the many valuable exchanges of information and techniques we share in her office.

Drs. Scott and Deb Walker, at whose excellent NET seminars and workshops I learned so much.

Marilyn Gordon and Stephanie Rothman, for all that I gain while participating in their e-groups.

Pat McCallum who first introduced me to "releasing" through her processes and book on Essence Repatterning.

Diana Keel, an attorney as well as gifted healer, who first taught me "tapping" and advanced muscle testing techniques.

Gary Craig, developer of EFT, who introduced me to the Association for Comprehensive Energy Psychology (ACEP) and tirelessly creates more awareness of this new field of healing.

With Love,

Beverly Nadler

VIBRATIONAL HARMONY

Table of Contents

Acknowledgements	
Preface - Why Read This Book	1
Forward -- Joyce E. Barrie	3
Introduction – John F. Demartini	4
1. The Epiphany That Led to This Book	5
2. Why We Don't Get What We Want	7
3. Intentions of This Book	13
4. How Paradigms Work	15
5. The Paradigm That Runs Us	18
6. Breaking Through the Accepted Paradigm	21
7. Amazing People Who Do Extraordinary Things	27
8. A New Paradigm – The "Energy" Model	30
9. The Laws of Attraction and Vibration	37
10. Coincidences and Synchronicity	41
11. The Laws of Polarity and Rhythm	46
12. The Law of Cause and Effect	52
13. How the Human Mind Works	54
14. The Superconscious – Your Infallible Guide	62
15. Understanding Your Feelings and Emotions	64
16. Programming the Subconscious Mind	70
17. The Technology of Reprogramming	72
18. Why the Subconscious Resists Reprogramming	76

19. The "Magic" of Energy Psychology	78
20. Basic Release Process for Letting Go of Negativity	85
21. Differences Between the Material and Energy Models	90
22. How to Reprogram Your Mind to Accept the Energy Model	94
23. The Importance of Loving Yourself	97
24. How to Create Self-Love	102
25. Releasing Negatives As They Come Up	108
26. Reprogramming for Health, Money and Whatever You Want	112
27. Integrating New Programming Into Your Daily Life	122
28. The Healing Power of Your Breath	125
29. The Challenge of Reprogramming	127
30. Faith, Confidence and Belief	134
31. How to Create Faith	142
32. Physical Things *Do* Matter	147
33. Achieving Vibrational Harmony	148
34. Remember These Points	155
An Open Letter from my Heart to my Readers	158
You Can Live Your Vision (Poem)	160
Programs and Speaking Information	161
Resources -- Books, Tapes, etc.	163
Order Form	167
About Beverly	168

PREFACE -- WHY READ THIS BOOK
by the Author

As I write this preface to the new edition, I am aware that never in our history has it been more important for people to know the spiritual and mental laws that govern our universe. Recently, the United States was the target of devastating terrorist attacks, and the *only* way people can make sense out of this tragedy is to understand how these laws operate. There is nothing that can explain these events -- especially if there is a loving God and a universe that supports us -- *except the laws*. Likewise, it is the *application* of these laws that can help us restore order, out of the chaos, to our lives.

The universal laws can be compared to the 'rules' of the "game of life." Although it is vital to know the rules when embarking on any endeavor, the rules for creating the life we desire are not generally taught...at least not in a *simple* format that clearly explains **why** and **how** things happen as they do.

Personal growth teachings and success philosophies tell us that our life is the result of the way we use our mind, and no one involved in self-development disputes this. However, though we learn many powerful techniques to improve our lives, if we don't understand how these laws operate, the techniques are often difficult, even seemingly impossible, to apply. When we do our best and things don't improve (or perhaps they get worse), we become disillusioned and discouraged -- wondering why "it" isn't working.

Hopefully, we will not have to continue dealing with anything as tragic as the recent events. However, life still has its share of personal calamities, plus natural disasters – volcanoes, earthquakes, tornadoes, hurricanes, etc. While we may realize these are part of "nature", if we lose loved ones or we are injured or our property and livelihood are destroyed, we painfully ask "Why? Why me? Why them?"

How life actually "works" -- including why 'bad' things happen to good people and good things happen to 'bad' people -- can only be explained by the universal laws and *vibrational harmony*. This knowledge, plus knowing how the human mind functions and having effective techniques for making desired changes and dealing with life's traumas, gives you much more control of your own life. When you can't figure out why things happen as they do, you often blame yourself. Knowing how life works restores your faith – especially faith in *yourself*.

Discovering there really ARE laws, and learning how they operate, is the first step to creating the life you desire. Understanding your mind and learning how to reprogram your subconscious (your mental computer) is the next step.

"Vibrational Harmony" gives you the *foundation* for change, growth, healing and success and empowers you in all aspects of your life…regardless of outer circumstances.

September 12, 2001

FOREWORD
by Joyce E. Barrie

A remarkable book by a remarkable woman. I am truly excited, inspired, motivated and empowered by "Vibrational Harmony", Beverly Nadler's latest book. When we truly understand how the laws of the universe work, coupled with an understanding of the programming that runs us, we are on the way to a happier, more fulfilled life.

I know of no greater author, teacher and trainer that can bring home these universal truths in a way that equips us with the tools we need to make our lives so much better. Beverly Nadler is someone I am proud to call my friend. She excels at whatever she undertakes.

One need only look at any of several books she has written to know that her words of wisdom are a gift to us all. (I had the privilege of co-authoring a book with her and two other people – "How to Get What You Want"...The Secrets of Having More Love, Health and Money!") One need only attend her Cabaret shows to see her talent as a singer and performer. One need only read her poetry to see her natural rhythm for life itself. One need only read her Live Your Vision newsletters to appreciate how articulate and informative Beverly is.

I really have great vibrations about "Vibrational Harmony", a book you do not put down when you want to affirm how to stay up about life.

Joyce E. Barrie
Personal & Professional Success Coach
Trainer, Author
Founder and Creator, The Humor Playshop
New York, NY

INTRODUCTION
by Dr. John F. Demartini

Since I was a teenager I dreamed of becoming a master of life. I have been on a quest for clarity of mission, inspired action and poised body and mind. Along my journey I have come upon many master teachers. One such special being is Beverly Nadler. I met her eighteen years ago, and from that moment until today her encouraging words have inspired me.

Her teachings and writings have led and challenged me to ever greater vision and action. Her dedicated study of the laws of the universe, as they relate to self-mastery, are signs of her commitment to humanity. She has found the philosopher's stone, the essence, the elixir, the principles that will stand the tests of time -- those mysterious truths that awaken greatness, that help make immortals out of mortals.

Her special new book entitled "Vibrational Harmony" is a gem that glimmers with insight, sparkles with beauty and sizzles with wisdom. We are all here to shine, but we all certainly require some polish. Beverly's wisdom and secrets of self-mastery will buff the rough edges off your present life and let you radiate with new and elevated actions and vibrations. It is simply a must in any serious seeker's personal development library.

Dr. John F. Demartini
Best selling author,
    Count Your Blessings - The Healing Power of Gratitude and Love
Founder,
    The Concourse of Wisdom School of Philosophy and Healing
Houston, Texas

Chapter 1

THE "EPIPHANY" THAT LED TO THIS BOOK

Epiphany is defined as a "flash of insight", "a sudden intuitive understanding". And that is exactly what happened to me! That's what this book is about.

When I had my epiphany, I started to write an article, and it just grew and grew -- like Pinocchio's nose, except it wasn't because of a lie. It was because of a truth – a truth so powerful, so compelling, that it could not be contained in an article. It had to be a book. Let me tell you how I came to write it.

Over the last two decades, the self-help/personal growth movement has mushroomed. There are countless books, tapes and trainings on psychology, philosophy, spirituality, personal growth, metaphysics, natural healing, relationships, goal-setting, how to create success, the power of faith and belief, handling emotions, energy healing, prayer, spiritual principles, intuition, mental imagery, affirmations, meditation – the list of subjects and titles is almost endless.

Yet, I felt something was missing. There was no book that

correlated and integrated the many diverse and often conflicting teachings so that people could readily see the "threads of truth" that run through and unify them all. No teaching seemed to clearly show the relationship between what people *want* in life, the natural *laws* that govern our universe, the way we *think and feel*, our *subconscious beliefs* and what we actually *get*.

Though there was no end to the self-help material, many people couldn't figure out *how to apply* what they learned to the everyday challenges and demands of their life-style, health, career, family life and financial issues. There were many gaps and missing links that confused them.

For months I had been pondering over my work, trying to figure out how I could explain that this teaching is "different", that it fills in these gaps and missing links. With all the excellent books on the market, how could I get that message across? I knew there had to be a way, but it eluded me…until one day, as I sat at my computer clicking away, the "epiphany" came.

I was startled by my own realization. I had made a discovery that, when understood, can impact upon the lives of people involved in their own personal or professional growth in ways so magical, we cannot even imagine them. *That discovery – and all that is implicit within it -- is what this book is about.*

Chapter 2

WHY WE DON'T GET WHAT WE WANT

Billions of dollars are spent annually on books, tapes, seminars, retreats and special trainings and events. Companies and organizations invest a tremendous amount of money to hire excellent inspiring, motivating speakers, trainers and coaches, in an effort to change their managers and mid-level employees from the inside out.

Though there has been an unprecedented interest in all things connected with personal growth, spirituality, natural healing and business and professional success, far too many people are not experiencing the long-term changes and results they seek and expect. The question is "Why"? This book not only answers that question, it tells you what you can *do* about it. It tells you *how* to get what you want.

At first I thought that the reason people are not getting what they want is because they are overwhelmed and bewildered by so much material – or confused by what appear to be contradictions among the many valuable teachings. But that's only part of the answer. Here's the *real* answer:

The new information and techniques for change are not based upon the paradigm that we have accepted as "the truth" for centuries. They are based upon a *new* paradigm -- one that is unknown to most people.

And the fact is, we can't successfully use new paradigm information and tools within the old paradigm structure. That's like trying to put round pegs into square holes.

The dictionary defines "paradigm" as a model. "Model" has numerous definitions, and the ones that best describe its meaning are: pattern, guide to be strictly followed, a standard established for use as a rule.

When we accept a paradigm, it is like a lens through which we view a part of the world (or the whole world) and it represents reality to us – whether it is true or false. In this case, the paradigm is about our concept of the *entire universe* and everything in it.

The one we have accepted for centuries, without ever questioning it, is the **Material Model**. This model tells us that things and conditions are solid and stable and *cannot be changed*. As long as we accept this model as the truth, even unknowingly, we are unable to make long-term changes in some areas of our lives, no matter what we do.

The **Material Model** has been such an integral part of our conditioning for so long that the vast majority of people believe it's "just the way things are", even though science has proven that it is *not* true. The truth is, things and conditions are *not* solid and unchangeable; in fact, everything is *always* in a state of change.

Since this incorrect belief has been accepted by humanity for centuries, the vast majority of people also believe (subconsciously, if not on a conscious level) that the changes they desire and are trying to make in their life are extremely difficult, if not impossible, to achieve. The reason this paradigm has such a powerful effect upon us is because it is *the major program* in our subconscious mind.

What Are Programs in the Subconscious?

Programs, as they are referred to in this book, are *instructions* in the subconscious, which is the computer-like part of the mind. Just as the programs in an electronic computer determine results and outcomes, so do the programs in your subconscious mind (your mental computer), only they are far more important. These programs determine the results and outcomes of *your life*.

The idea that the human brain and mind function like a highly sophisticated computer is difficult for some people to accept, especially those who prefer to focus on humanity's spiritual essence. However, as you will see in this book, there is no conflict; our spirituality co-exists with our programming. Award-winning cognitive researcher and acclaimed science writer, Steven Pinker, director of the Center for Cognitive Neuroscience at the Massachusetts Institute of Technology, confirms the computer-like operation of our brain and mind in his book "How the Mind Works".

What Are These Programs *For*?

Your programs give the directions for running your body. They keep your heart beating, your lungs breathing, your stomach digesting food, etc., without you consciously doing anything. In addition to programs for health and body functions, you have programs about your career, money and relationships, plus programs that define your skills and abilities. Your programs establish your limits and tell you what you can and can't do, have or be.

You are programmed with many beliefs about yourself (self-image and self-worth) and the universe (it's a friendly or a scary place…and anything in between). These beliefs become your reality because beliefs and programs are one and the same. Your mental computer (subconscious mind) does not care whether your programs are to your advantage or detriment. It carries them out the same as an electronic computer carries out its programs.

Let's say you have a belief (program) that no matter what you do, it's never good enough. You may actually do a great job, but you won't think so, and won't be satisfied. You are also likely to have people in your life who are never satisfied, don't appreciate you and probably take advantage of you. This scenario will play out indefinitely unless YOU change your program. (Yes, this book will show you how.)

Why Breakthroughs Don't Usually Last

Many people have the exhilarating experience of attending enlightening, inspiring, motivating personal growth and spiritual trainings that break through the barriers of their mind. They do firewalks and have amazing and important insights at seminars and workshops. They go off to retreats and come back feeling their life has transformed. They attend corporate trainings that have a tremendous impact upon them.

And yet, for most people, the marvelous experience and the valuable teachings fade away -- sometimes in as quickly as a few days. It is almost as if it never happened. Why? *Because the mind goes back to its old programs.* You might say your mental computer returns to its "default" position in the same way that your electronic computer sometimes goes back to default, even when you don't want it to.

The breakthroughs, as significant and as real as they were, did not last because the new information, techniques, behaviors and insights were not sufficiently reinforced and the old programming took over again. This explains why people go from one powerful teaching to another, to another, to another – wondering why the magic doesn't remain.

It is not the fault of the teacher whose seminar, workshop or training is usually enlightening and offers valuable information, positive recommendations and action steps. Nor is it even the fault of the student. *It is because of the way the subconscious mind and its programming operate.*

This book will help you understand the workings of your mind and give you information, tools and techniques so that your breakthroughs can be permanent. With this new knowledge and understanding, every seminar or program you benefit from in the future and every enlightening book you read and tape you listen to that has to do with growth, healing, change and success will have more meaning. Every valuable tool and technique you learn and use in the future (including ones you've already learned) will be more empowering and effective, once you know *why* they work.

Your subconscious programs are always operating and they determine your thoughts, feelings, attitudes, perceptions and behaviors. Not only that, as you will learn, people, things, events, experiences and situations are actually drawn to you *because of* your programs. Your positive programs/beliefs help you get what you want. Your negative ones stop you.

This book will show you *why* your life is controlled by your programming, and how to *reprogram* yourself to get what you want. But first we'll look at why things happen as they do and how paradigms you accept as "the truth" affect your life.

Chapter 3

INTENTIONS OF THIS BOOK

My first intention in writing this book is to clear up confusion about how life actually "works". The universal laws – the spiritual and mental laws that govern every aspect of our lives -- explain this, and nothing else does. They are the "rules of the game of life", the *foundation* upon which all change, growth, success and healing are based. Trying to create the life you desire, without knowing these laws, is like trying to write and spell without knowing the alphabet.

This book will show you the relationship between the universal laws, what you want in life, the way you use your mind, your subconscious programs and what you actually *get*. Many people on a spiritual path don't feel they need this information. However, it is possible that knowing these laws, together with understanding how the mind works and being able to consciously change our programs, may be an *essential* step in the evolution of consciousness. Perhaps skipping this step is like skipping the step of crawling, which can interfere with physical and neurological development. (Many children who didn't crawl as babies must be "re-patterned" with a series of painstaking crawling exercises.) The knowledge in this book is for everyone -- from novice to long-time seeker.

My next, just as important, intention is to present the revolutionary concept that the paradigm humanity has accepted, the **Material Model**, is also the *operating system for our mental computer* (the subconscious mind) and it is largely responsible for the difficulties we have with change. You will understand why some of your efforts to make changes have often been met with frustration and struggle, and why you resist the inevitable changes you don't want. Are you resisting the rapid and often overwhelming (for many people) changes in technology and communication, perhaps? Or changes that are taking place where you work? Are you resisting ending a relationship that is clearly over?

You will learn about the new paradigm that is waiting to take over, a paradigm that allows change to take place with ease -- the **Energy Model**. You will see the enormous difference between the **Material Model** that makes change and growth painful and slow and the **Energy Model** that makes change and growth a pleasant experience. It is also my intention to share empowering tools and techniques for reprogramming yourself so you can get what you want -- beginning with programming yourself to accept the **Energy Model** as *your* operating system.

If you've invested much time, effort and money in your own personal and professional growth and have not yet had the results you anticipated, be assured that there's nothing wrong with you; you've just been missing vital information -- information that you're about to discover.

Chapter 4

HOW PARADIGMS WORK

We live with many paradigms. These are models and patterns we strictly follow, often without awareness. They become rules for our life and we follow them meticulously, even when they are unconscious. In fact, the more unconscious they are, the more we follow them.

Let me give you an idea of a paradigm and how it affects people's lives. Let's say a man wants to get married. His paradigm of marriage comes from his parents and grandparents – the good old-fashioned model where the husband works hard and supports his family while the wife is expected to make a comfortable, loving home for her husband and children.

Part of that paradigm includes a delicious dinner waiting for the husband when he comes home from work, and while he relaxes after dinner, his wife and children clean up. Usually within this model the husband is "in charge", so when there is a disagreement, the wife defers to the husband's decisions. A man who has this as his paradigm is convinced this is the "right way" (probably the only way) for a couple to have a harmonious, loving marriage relationship.

Now, he meets and falls in love with a woman who has a totally different paradigm. She loves her career and easily supports herself. In her model (paradigm), the woman works if she chooses, unless or until she decides she wants a child. Dinner is a joint venture; either they eat out or both participate in the cooking and cleaning up. No one is in charge, and when there is disagreement, they discuss the issues and negotiate until they are satisfied. Both believe their models of married life are "correct".

What's the likelihood of this couple having a good marriage?

The Paradigm We Accept "Runs" Our Life

I used the above example to show you that what we call "right" or "the truth" comes from our paradigms. The model we accept as real is like the lens through which we view and form our opinions about everything that is connected with specific areas of our lives. When it is an *all-inclusive* paradigm about how life works, it is the lens through which we view *everything* about ourselves, our lives and the entire world. Therefore, the model that represents reality to us dictates our perceptions, beliefs, thoughts, feelings, behaviors and actions. In short, it becomes the operating system of each individual's mental computer.

As such, it is to your life what the operating system of your electronic computer is to your computer. If you have a PC (personal computer) you know that a PC's operating system (such as Microsoft Windows 2000 or MAC OS8.6) runs the computer. *Every* program is dependent upon the operating system because it determines how all the other programs work. This is true, both in your electronic computer and your mental computer. That's why the operating system of your mental computer (your subconscious mind) affects every area of your life.

In Chapter 8, which explains the Energy Model in detail, you will see that science now confirms what ancient wisdom has taught for centuries. It is only since quantum physics revealed some of its theories that we can understand how the Energy Model completely alters our view of the universe and our relationship to it. While theories of quantum physics continually change as new discoveries confound even the most brilliant scientists on the planet, we (you and I) are concerned with only one theory…the one that tells us that we live in a **"unified field of energy"**.

Being aware that energy is all there is, and understanding how energy operates, inspires us to do what it takes to let go of the Material Model and accept the Energy Model as our operating system. Once we do this and learn to live in harmony with the laws of energy, we make sense out of our lives and our universe. What's more, we also have new tools to help us enjoy greater success, health and prosperity.

Chapter 5

THE PARADIGM THAT RUNS US

For centuries, the paradigm that has dominated our entire civilization has been the Material Model. It is so broad and far-reaching that it affects and influences every area and aspect of our life, and to some degree, no one is untouched by it. Even if we don't personally accept it, the people in our lives – people we live, work, play and communicate with -- do, and that influences how they respond to us and how we interact.

Humanity has lived with the Material Model for so long that we just take it for granted. When I use the word "material", it has nothing to do with money or greed. I am referring to a model of life based upon the concept of "matter" rather than the concept of "energy". There is a huge difference between the two models and how they impact upon us.

According to the Material Model, things and conditions are solid and stable, and we have little, if any, power to change them. This belief totally dis-empowers us. Yet, this is what most humans have been conditioned to believe. Even if we don't believe it on a conscious level, it is likely to be programmed into our subconscious, because it is part of *mass mind consciousness* (also called race-mind, collective unconscious, collective consciousness).

When we live our lives – consciously or unconsciously – from a basic program that says change is not possible, we automatically *resist* all changes we don't want and we *struggle* and often fight a losing battle when we try to make the changes we desire.

Perhaps you are one of the many people involved in self-help and personal growth who has wondered why, in spite of your strong intentions and efforts to make changes in some areas of your life -- to eat healthier, to stop smoking, to start exercising, to earn more money, to change your career, to improve your relationships, etc. -- you are often thwarted. Now you know a major reason: **your desire to change is in conflict with your mental computer's operating system, the Material Model.**

The new paradigm we are shifting to, the Energy Model, restores your power, for it recognizes that *everything* can be changed, and *is* always changing. The Energy Model is so empowering that when it becomes your operating system and you learn the laws of energy, you are able to attain what you want to be, do and have. Under this paradigm, you can transform your life, even to the point of creating what the rest of the world calls "miracles".

The Energy Model has been easing its way into the mass

consciousness for the last 30-40 years, and based upon market indicators, it is likely to replace the old paradigm in about 10 years. It takes a long time to change the collective consciousness. For instance, at one time it was believed that the earth was the center of the universe, and Galileo was almost put to death for declaring the sun did not revolve around the earth. To save his life, he had to deny his truth. People resisted using phones, riding in cars, and flying in airplanes for years after they were proven to be safe and efficient means of communication and transportation.

Our paradigms set our limits and boundaries. Today, a large percentage of the public still suffers from chronic diseases when they could be helped and even healed with natural methods of health care, such as chiropractic, acupuncture, homeopathy, various forms of "energy healing", nutrition, herbs, etc. But they won't even explore these possibilities because they are stuck in the paradigm of the Material Model, and the medical model is an intrinsic part of that paradigm. This explains why people can read or hear about, and even witness, other people's remarkable recoveries through natural health therapies and treatments, but they still won't use them. Maybe they will in 10 years.

This book is for people like you, who are not willing to wait another 10 years to become, do and have what they want in life.

Chapter 6

BREAKING THROUGH THE ACCEPTED PARADIGM

Humanity seemed quite content with the Material Model for centuries. Then, in the 1960s, a significant number of people began to awaken to their own potential and realized there was more to life than that which they could see and touch. By the 70s, a magnificent movement towards personal evolvement and spiritual growth was well under way.

The movement has continuously grown, and since the 80s, more and more individuals and companies have been seriously pursuing personal and professional success, better health (physical, mental and emotional), spiritual growth and greater prosperity. Many are also searching for their "mission" in life as they pursue their goals.

While inspiring and motivating speakers and authors -- including Mark Victor Hansen, Jack Canfield, Tony Robbins, Dr. Wayne Dyer, Dr. Deepok Chopra, Stephen Covey, Dennis Waitely and others -- have made a tremendous impact on the lives of countless people, some individuals break free of all limitations, focus on their dreams and turn them into reality *without* books, tapes and seminars.

They create wealth and accomplish feats even beyond their own wildest dreams, and they never heard of the Material Model or the Energy Model and know nothing about subconscious programming. Superstar entertainers and athletes are certainly in that category. Barbra Streisand, Madonna and Michael Jordan are examples of people who came from meager backgrounds and reinvented themselves to go for and achieve their dreams.

Their *passion* for what they wanted to do and their *belief* in themselves overcame the kind of programming that often results from lack of money and/or a difficult childhood. And they achieved unimaginable wealth and fame in the process.

What's Their Magic Formula?

If you are wondering what their "magic formula" was and is – it is probably something like this: **they always had unwavering faith in themselves and their ability to accomplish what they wanted. And nothing on the outside could disturb their vision on the inside.**

The main message in self-help, personal growth and success teachings has always been "change the way you think." People who have unwavering faith, regardless of outer conditions, do not have to change the way they think. For whatever reasons, among all the messages programmed into their subconscious in childhood, there was a powerful belief in *themselves* (and probably in God). This program gives them "the faith that moves mountains", and from that faith comes the willingness, determination, commitment and ability to do whatever is necessary to fulfill their dreams. Oprah is one of those people who had faith in herself and in God, in spite of living in poverty and being sexually abused as a child. She is the epitome of success and a beloved inspiration to millions of people – even though she is a black, full-figured female in a white, skinny, male-dominated industry.

I mention famous people because everyone knows their names. There are non-celebrities who believe in themselves and passionately go for their dreams and achieve their goals. However, people who do not have that level of faith often have a different experience, no matter how hard they work and how much they want success.

That's because when that kind of belief in ourselves and our dream is not a natural part of who-we-are, we need to reprogram ourselves. However, when we try, we keep coming up against an operating system (the Material Model) in our mental computer that makes change seemingly impossible or extremely challenging. In addition, the most effective tools and techniques for change are based on the Energy Model, and that paradigm is not yet a part of most people's consciousness. Therefore, we often aren't able to use the tools effectively.

Until humanity's paradigm shifts to the new paradigm, it will continue to be difficult to use the new energy-based tools and techniques. Of course, that doesn't have to affect you. By reprogramming your mind, the Energy Model can become *your* operating system, and you will be able to make the changes necessary for you to achieve your goals.

How the Subconscious Mind Learns

In order to impress anything new or different upon the subconscious – whether it's new communication techniques, new business procedures, a new exercise program, new skills, new habits of action or thought OR new information to change fundamental beliefs – your subconscious needs continuous *repetition and reinforcement*.

While it is possible to have an "awakening" (such as the alcoholic has when he proclaims: "I saw God, and I don't have to drink anymore", and gives up alcohol), this is rare. Usually it takes a great deal of repetition and reinforcement for permanent change to take place. Think of anything you've ever learned – how to spell and read, add and subtract, ride a bike, play an instrument, drive a car, operate a computer, etc. -- you did it over and over and over, until it became a habit.

People who have natural talents take to certain activities "like a duck takes to water". But even they repeat and reinforce their skills to become more proficient or outstanding. (We call it "practice".) Ask any athlete, entertainer or successful business person. The top golfer in the world, Tiger Woods, continuously works to become even better.

How Do We Let Go of the Old Paradigm?

The way to let go of an old paradigm is to replace it with a new one. Nature abhors a vacuum, so if we try to let go of the old paradigm without giving ourselves a new one, we still keep running up against the old one.

Before we can accept the Energy Model as our paradigm, we have to know how it operates. We need information about this model -- information that makes sense to us on a conscious level; otherwise we automatically reject it. The information must be repeated and reinforced until the subconscious believes it, just as it now believes the Material Model is true.

Self-help teachings tell us it is as important to feed our mind every day as it is to feed our body. They tell us to read and listen to inspiring, motivating material daily in order to impress our subconscious with positive messages. Most of us find other people's stories inspiring and compelling. We are fascinated by true tales of people who go from rags to riches, failure to success, sickness to health, victim to victor -- and we love to read and hear these kinds of stories over and over again. Why?

Because we hope that if we read and hear enough of them, often enough, our subconscious will believe that we can do these things also – that we can go from rags to riches, failure to success, sickness to health, victim to victor. As we read and listen to these stories with fascination and wonder, we repeat a silent prayer, *"Me too; why not me too?"*

In the chapter that follows you will read about some of the most inspiring people I know of. However, as gratifying as it is to learn about other people's success, especially in the midst of trauma and challenges, is it not of great benefit to know *how* and *why* they are able to do what they do – the actual laws they invoke (often without their awareness), laws that govern us, laws that are the *foundation* for our lives?

Because I'm convinced it is, you will soon read about the universal and mental laws and how they operate and interact in your life. There are many wonderful books filled with astonishing, awe-inspiring stories, such as the phenomenally successful "Chicken Soup for the Soul" series; read and enjoy them. This book shows you the principles *behind* the stories, so you can deliberately create your own miracles.

It is said, *"Know the truth and the truth shall set you free"*. The Energy Model of life is "the truth" and it sets you free when you program it into your consciousness with the same dedication most people put into planning a vacation. The Energy Model sets you free when you believe it, not only on a conscious level, but on a subconscious level as well. Once it is accepted by your subconscious, it becomes your operating system and allows you to break through past limitations and reprogram yourself. That's how you get what you want.

Chapter 7

AMAZING PEOPLE WHO DO EXTRAORDINARY THINGS

When we are born with specific talents – in art, dance, music, technology, business, sports, etc. – it means we have been programmed with these abilities from birth. Because of our natural talents, our subconscious has instructions for us to do certain things with ease. Our mind says, "I can do that", and we can.

There are people, however, who don't have natural, in-born talents in certain directions and through their own efforts, become far more masterful than those who do. I am not just referring to people who don't have an inborn aptitude for something in which they train themselves to excel. The people in this chapter have far greater challenges.

Mouth and Foot Painting Artists

For instance, there are amazing people who, due to traumatic accidents, are disabled and have no use of their hands -- yet become extraordinary artists. They are Foot and Mouth Painting Artists, whose stunning works of art, painted by holding a brush between their toes or in their mouth, appear on greeting cards and calendars. Their art rivals the beauty, detail and elegance of the finest paintings of talented Hallmark Cards artists, and their original artwork could easily hang in quality galleries.

My introduction to these artists came when I received a mailing, and on the envelope was a photo of a woman with a paintbrush in her mouth. Next to the picture were her words, "Painting is how I show my love for life!" I remember looking at that envelope in a state of shock, wondering how anyone could feel that way, in the midst of what I considered to be great suffering.

As far as I know, no one is born with a talent to paint with his or her feet or mouth. These amazing artists developed this skill because of their determination to have a purpose in life. They totally reprogrammed themselves in several areas: They developed and perfected a talent they were not born with, after first creating a mental state that allowed them to let go of anger, resentment and self-pity and the belief that their life was useless and worthless, and they went beyond acceptance of their life to become an inspiration to others.

Handicapped Athletes

The same is true of handicapped athletes who compete in major sports events, climb mountains without feet, ski without legs and accomplish other "impossible" feats. These people refuse to allow their disabilities to be a barrier in their life. In 1995, at the age of 26, Erik Weihenmayer climbed to the top of Mount McKinley, America's tallest mountain, even though he's blind. Rory McCarthy, a man in his forties with lower body muscular atrophy, cycles across the country and stays fit by handcycling, canoeing and kayaking.

Christopher Reeve

Of course, the person we're most familiar with is "Superman", Christopher Reeve, the handsome actor who was left paralyzed from a spinal cord injury after being thrown from his horse in a riding competition. This is a man whose life was defined by luxury, celebrity, wealth, success and all the "good things".

Aside from his external adjustments, what internal adjustments did he have to make? We will never know. But we know that he continues to successfully work at his craft, directing and acting in films, while very effectively using his celebrity status to bring greater awareness and support for the approximately 250,000 paralyzed people in the U.S.

We call these people and their accomplishments incredible – and they are. They probably never heard of any of the principles in this book, but at some level they absolutely *know* they can accomplish what they set out to do. They are all gifts to humanity, for they show us what human beings are capable of becoming and achieving.

Chapter 8

A NEW PARADIGM – THE "ENERGY MODEL"

The chapters that follow will help you understand many things that are considered mysterious. They are mysterious because they make no sense from the Material Model. They only make sense when you know the Energy Model.

This information comes from the discoveries of modern science and ancient esoteric teachings, called Hermetic Philosophy (the metaphysical teachings of Hermes Trismegistus, master Egyptian occultist). What you are about to learn is a brief synopsis of what was taught in the Mystery Schools in Egypt and Greece. It took many years for students to understand the basics that you will know before you finish this book. In ancient times, the teachings were only for members of royalty and religious, political and military leaders. To teach this to ordinary people – the masses – was not allowed. It could even mean being put to death!

There were two reasons for this. One was that the average person was not sufficiently evolved in consciousness to handle this knowledge wisely. The other was that the rulers did not want to lose their power. If the populace knew the truth, ordinary people would be able to achieve self-mastery, and would no longer agree to be controlled by their leaders and rulers.

Where Physics and Metaphysics Agree

Some people feel that metaphysics is a bit questionable and should not be compared to science. If you one of these people, it may interest you to know that much of modern physics is based on Aristotle's concepts, as described in his first great work called "The Physics". Later, when Aristotle concluded that the physical universe was formed out of a non-physical Source, he wrote another great work and called it "Metaphysics".

The word metaphysics means "above the physical" and tells us that we are dealing with non-physical realms. In case you think these realms don't exist, think again; your thoughts, feelings, emotions, soul and spirit are all non-physical.

According to quantum physics, the entire universe is a *unified field of energy*. This means everything that exists, including you, is energy. Furthermore, everything that exists comes out of, or is created from, this unified (one) energy field. Quantum physics also tells us that this energy is intelligent, or *conscious*. To be conscious means to have the ability to respond to stimuli, an ability even sub-atomic particles possess.

In the metaphysical Mystery Schools -- also called

Wisdom Schools and Esoteric (secret) Schools -- students were taught that there is one consciousness in the universe, that everything that exists comes out of this one consciousness, and this consciousness is *intelligent*. (You may recognize that many religions and spiritual teachings agree with this.)

Sounds like science and metaphysics are both saying the same thing, doesn't it? The power of this energy or consciousness (which we call God, Jehovah, Allah, Brahma, Lord and hundreds of other names in different cultures) is enormous. We first became aware of how enormous when an atom bomb was dropped on Hiroshima in 1945. We could not see the energy in the bomb, but we witnessed its power.

Physicists claim that the energy within each cubic centimeter of space is so great that it is greater than the total energy of all the matter in the known universe, or the equivalent of a trillion atomic bombs. Just think of it -- this enormous power resides in YOU! It can be used to build and to destroy. With knowledge, you can build the life you want.

Am I saying that God and Energy are one and the same? Since it is not for the finite mind to understand the Infinite, I don't have the answer. What I *do* know is that God (or whatever name you give to the Power that created all-that-exists) is in every speck of Its creation. Whatever this Power is that gave rise to the Universe, It *uses* energy and the laws of energy in order to create and govern Its creation. We humans, created in the image and likeness of this Power (remember that from the old testament?), must learn how to use this *same* energy to create what we want in our lives.

Attributes of Energy

The following is not a physics lesson. It is information about energy and its laws that will help you become a conscious creator (really "co-creator", creating with the Creator) of your own life.

- Energy cannot be created or destroyed. It can only be *changed*...and it is always changing.

- Energy expresses on all levels – spiritual, mental and physical. The spiritual level is the realm of ideas and images. The mental level is the realm of thoughts, feelings and emotions. The physical level is the realm of things and actions.

- Energy is *electro-magnetic* and in a constant state of *vibration*, with each form of energy vibrating at its own specific rate or *speed*. The rate is a measurement called *frequency*. The higher the frequency, the faster the speed of the vibration.

- *Everything* is energy. Einstein's theory of relativity, $E=MC2$ – which means "energy equals matter times the velocity of light squared" -- tells us that *energy and matter are the same*. Matter *appears* solid, but that's because it's vibrating at a very low frequency. Energy consists of waves and particles in continuous vibration. If you examine any solid object (matter) under a high-powered microscope, you'll see electrons (negatively charged particles) and protons (positively charged particles) whirling in tons and tons of empty space, doing a cosmic dance. You would have visual proof that nothing is solid.

- The *appearance* of solidity, along with the fact that until a few decades ago the concept of a "unified field of energy" did not exist, has kept humanity believing in the Material Model.

Regarding matter, this is what Einstein said in the latter years of his life, when he was questioned about the desirability of studying metaphysics: "Anyone who pursues physics far enough is eventually forced into metaphysics because if we examine matter closely enough it disappears and *we find nothing but a frequency of vibration.*" (The italics are mine.)

Here's what all this means to you. Since all forms of energy vibrate, are electro-magnetic – that is, attract and repel other forms of energy – and can be changed, it means *you* are vibrating energy, always attracting and repelling other forms of energy (i.e: people, things, conditions, circumstances, situations and events) and *you can makes changes in yourself and in your life.* It also means that every person and thing in the universe has these same attributes and qualities and has the ability to change. Furthermore, whether we like it or not, changes are always happening. Often these are changes we do not choose, do not like, do not want and try to resist.

Explaining the Unexplainable

The Energy Model is the only model that explains the "unexplainable." Coincidences, synchronicity, spontaneous healing, psychic phenomena, intuition, instantaneous dislike or rapport with someone, the power of the mind, the value of hypnosis, the importance of faith and gratitude, prayers that are answered and prayers that are not answered, bad things happening to good people and good things happening to bad people, being in the right place at the right time, and things that are considered mystical and mysterious can be understood *only* within the context of the Energy Model.

We Are Energy Beings

Healing can best be understood when we know we are *energy* beings, that our bodies are *self-healing*, that all healing comes from *within* and -- because of the body-mind energy connection -- thoughts and feelings affect our health.

Only when we know about energy and vibrations, do we care about auras, chakras and meridian lines and points, do we recognize the benefits of disciplines like yoga, tai chi and chi gong, or does it make sense that people can be healed by non-medical methods -- such as chiropractic, acupuncture, naturopathy, etc., and with live foods, whole food supplements, herbs, essential oils, homeopathic remedies, Bach flowers, light, color, music and certain sounds and the touch and "vibrations" of people with positive energy fields.

All of the above have high frequency vibrations that are in harmony with health. This makes no sense from the Material Model, but it fits into the Energy Model. The Energy Model also explains why people claim astonishing changes occur in their lives because of feng shui, a Chinese system for creating a harmonious flow of energy in any environment.

Everyone Has the Right To Know

It saddens me to read or hear people talk about health issues and other challenges that could be alleviated if the public knew of, understood and accepted the Energy Model. This would motivate more people to seek and find the right energy-based products, therapies and/or services for them.

Health professionals whose modalities are energy-based (rather than drug-based) would barely have time for all the people who want to see them, and products that help change people's energy field and vibrations would fly off the shelves. Unfortunately, most people do not have this knowledge...yet.

On the following pages you'll learn more about the laws of energy and vibrational harmony.

Chapter 9

THE LAWS OF ATTRACTION AND VIBRATION

The Energy Model tells us that energy is electro-magnetic and we get what we get in life by attracting what we are in vibrational harmony (also called "resonance") with. What determines vibrational harmony? Whatever you focus your attention upon, *consciously or unconsciously* -- whether wanted or unwanted -- puts you in vibrational harmony with it. When you are in vibrational harmony with what you want, it is drawn to you by magnetic attraction.

The Law of Attraction

Here's how it works: Your energy field, composed primarily of mental vibrations, radiates into the universe and by Law of Attraction, attracts to you, or attracts you to, people, things, conditions, situations, events and experiences that you are in resonance with. These become your life. We've been taught that we attract with our thoughts, but we really attract with our vibrations. Most of what we call "thoughts" are not thoughts, anyhow. They are emotionally charged *automatic reactions* coming from subconscious programs. These automatic reactions vibrate at specific frequencies and attract back to us the components they are in harmony with -- and these become our life.

Because most people who are involved in personal growth believe in the power of the mind, they spend a certain amount of time (usually ten to thirty minutes a day) consciously focusing on what they want. They may do this by repeating affirmations, creating mental images, meditating and/or saying positive prayers. However, unless people monitor *all* their thoughts and conversations, it is likely that the rest of the day their vibrations are coming from their programming. If their programs are positive, their thoughts are positive and so are their vibrations.

Negative programs, however, produce negative thoughts like criticism, intolerance, judgments, self-condemnation, etc. Negative thoughts cause worry, guilt, anxiety, frustration and feelings of fear, sadness, anger, hatred, resentment, etc. These emotions, though they are all part of being human, vibrate at a low frequency. If we stay in a negative mental/emotional state, we put ourselves in harmony with negative people and things. These lead to undesired conditions, events and experiences, such as accidents, discord and illness.

While we are unlikely to avoid ever having negative (i.e: undesired) emotions, once we understand them (see Chapter 15), we can acknowledge, accept and embrace them, learn from their message, and then let them go.

Vibrational Harmony

The Law of Vibration

You are already familiar with one measurement of vibration called *frequency*. Vibrations have another measurement, which is called *amplitude*. While frequency is the rate or *speed* of the vibration, amplitude is the strength or *power* of the vibration.

As an illustration, think of a radio. All around the world millions of stations are broadcasting, probably dozens in your immediate area alone, all at their specific frequencies. Your radio, however, only picks up one broadcast, the one your radio is tuned to, or in *resonance* (vibrational harmony) with. You decide the station you want to hear by turning the station dial. You also decide the amplitude, or power of the vibration, by turning the volume up or down.

This is also the way life works. Everything vibrates; the scale goes from the lowest to the highest possible frequency. Every person, place and object, every sound and color, every condition, event and circumstance, every word and illustration on the page of a book – they are all in a continuous state of vibration.

There are countless vibrations vying for your attention, and you get to choose the ones you focus upon. You're in resonance with whatever you focus upon, just as if you chose a station on your radio dial. You determine how much energy you give to the object of your attention by your *concentration* and *emotion*. That's how you raise the amplitude.

Most people focus on what they *don't* want, and they do so with very high amplitude. They don't want sickness, but they talk about their aches and pains all the time, and they put themselves in resonance with more aches and pains. Most people want more money, but when they think about money, they think about the *lack* of money, and they vibrate in harmony with more lack — which is what they don't want. They choose "stations" (frequencies) they don't want and they raise the amplitude (power) on them. Can you see that a major reason why people don't get what they want is because they often have their attention on what they *don't* want?

Nature, beauty, art, classical music, certain sounds and objects that have harmony and balance all have high vibrations. That's why going to a museum, beach or park (preferably clean and un-crowded) or listening to a symphony is so satisfying. When our vibrations combine with these high frequencies they delight our soul, and raise *our* vibrations.

The Law of Attraction is always operating, and attracts to us people, conditions, situations and events that we are knowingly or unknowingly in vibrational harmony with. That's why it's important to *choose* the vibrations you radiate.

The next chapter gives you examples of the Laws of Attraction and Vibration in action, which we call coincidences or "being in synch".

Chapter 10

COINCIDENCES AND SYNCHRONICITY

The telephone rings. It's Laura. You pick it up. "Laura!" you say, "I was just thinking about you. How strange that you called."

Your baby is sleeping in another room down the hall from you. Suddenly, he wakes up, crying in pain. You go to his room. Nothing strange about that, except that you woke up and walked into the room a full 90 seconds *before* he awoke!

You need a piece of information for an important report you're writing. You just know you had it, but you've looked through all your files, and nothing turned up. You can't imagine how to get this information again. The next day, in the mail, you receive a brochure about a topic you thought was unrelated -- in fact, you almost threw the material away, but something said "read this". You did, and there on the second page is the exact piece of information you are seeking.

Your schedule, between work, family, appointments and other commitments is very difficult to handle, and now you've gotten yourself into an impossible situation. You scheduled several people at the same time. Who do you call? Who can you switch without them getting angry? Can someone else take your place? What should you do? You agonize over this a bit, and then let it go, deciding to make a decision the following day. When you return to your office the next day and listen to your phone messages, two of the people on your overbooked calendar are asking for rescheduling. How perfect!

Finding the Right Healer

You've been sick and in pain. Lately, you've been reading about natural "alternative" healing. You've begun to meditate and have even changed your diet. You're definitely feeling better, but you know there's more that can be done. Your friend, who lives in another state, recommends that you go to a chiropractor, one that is skillful in traditional chiropractic and also practices a specialized technique.

You've never been to a chiropractor. In fact, though you've heard they help people, you have no idea how to find a good one. The phone book? Everybody advertises as if he or she is "the best". You make a mental note to ask some of your friends and associates if they can recommend anyone. Imagine your surprise when you have lunch with a co-worker and he begins the conversation by raving about the chiropractor he went to yesterday. Not only is she good, she practices a very specialized technique. Wouldn't you know it, this is the technique your friend said to look for!

More Examples

You're ready to buy a car. After reading reports on cars in several magazines, you've decided on the make and model you want. You realize that you don't remember seeing this particular car much, recently. Hmm, does that mean no one is buying it? Is there something wrong with it? You begin to look for that model while you're driving. No sooner said than done. There's one. There's another one. Wow, there's another one. Suddenly it seems that lots of people are driving the same car you are thinking about buying.

You're going to a meeting and you're running late. As you rush down the highway, you accidentally get off at the wrong exit, and there's no way to get back on. You remember that you can get to your destination by using the side streets. You decide to go that way. You arrive in time for the meeting.

When you arrive, you're surprised to find that several people are not there, people who are usually prompt. While waiting for them to show up, you all listen to the news. You hear an announcement about a three-car accident on the highway you were on, just one exit after you got off. Delays are expected to be up to one hour. Weren't you lucky you made that mistake?

I could go on and on with these stories, but I'm sure you've got the point. How many of these situations, or ones that are similar, have happened to you? They are all what we call "coincidences", but coincidence is just the name given to synchronous events for which there is no logical explanation. They are really the Laws of Vibration and Attraction in operation.

How Do These Things Happen?

The dictionary defines *synchronize* as: "represent as; show to be coincident; simultaneous." It defines *synchronous* as: "happening at the same time; occurring together; simultaneous; having the same rate and phase, as *vibrations*" (emphasis is mine).

Synchronous events and coincidences occur because you and "it" -- the person, place, event or thing -- have harmonious vibrations or energy fields. In other words, you resonate at the same frequency, and by Law of Attraction, you are brought together simultaneously. As unbelievable as it may seem, *nothing* can come into your life unless, at some level, you and "it" are in resonance.

A mother has rapport with her baby and she internally responds to his call even before the call is made. Our thoughts vibrate out into the universe and are picked up, at the unconscious level, by people and conditions that vibrate in harmony with the thought energy we project. It's called resonance or *vibrational harmony*!

The next page tells of another kind of synchronicity.

What About Luck?

To me, luck is where persistence and opportunity meet. In business and in life this would translate as: "If you keep doing the best you can and you persist -- expecting to succeed -- opportunity will eventually knock."

While speaking to a group of actors in New York City, Jason Kravits, an actor who played a major character in an award-winning weekly TV show, said: *"The more you persist, the more opportunities show up."* Jason was the combative assistant D.A. everyone loved to hate on "The Practice", a role that expanded from two episodes to two seasons. I was very impressed with his philosophy, especially since he didn't know about the laws I teach...at least not consciously.

It seems "luck" happens when we persist and do our best at the work we love, controlling what we can without worrying about what we can't (that means we "keep the faith"). I call this kind of luck 'synchronicity'; Jason calls it 'karma' or magic. In reality, it's the Laws of Attraction and Vibration. In Jason's case, his persistence attracted a major role because he "happened" to be in the right place at the right time. Interestingly enough, while he was easily cast for that role, he had persisted and persisted for one he didn't get in a show that never made it to the network. Had he gotten that role, he would not have been able to audition for "The Practice".

Ah, the Lord (law) works in mysterious ways!

Chapter 11

THE LAWS OF POLARITY AND RHYTHM

The universal Laws of Polarity and Rhythm explain the paradoxes of life, and nothing else does. Most people, including many who are aware of the Laws of Vibration and Attraction, don't know how these two laws operate. They don't understand why "bad things happen to good people" (like them!). Lack of knowledge and understanding of the laws leaves them confused, frustrated and unhappy.

The Law of Polarity

This law tells us that everything in the universe has a polar opposite. In the dictionary, the word *polar* is defined as: "opposite in character, nature and direction."

Familiar polar opposites are: male/female, big/small, high/low, out/in, up/down, west/east, give/receive, fast/slow. We accept those opposites without judgment, but not these: pleasure/pain, rich/poor, health/disease, war/peace, chaos/order, good/evil, God/devil. We call polarities we like "good", and ones we don't like "bad". And we do everything we can to avoid what we consider bad.

In the spiritual realm, positive and negative are just polar opposites and have nothing to do with good and bad. They are opposite energies – positive/assertive/masculine energy and negative/receptive/feminine energy. Everything in the universe contains both. All of creation comes out of the joining of these two energies – the positive proton (+) and the negative electron (-). This is true in the atom, and in the mineral, plant, animal and human kingdoms, as well as in the spiritual realm. This is the Law of Gender, and the Oriental yin/yang symbol represents this universal principle.

The Law of Gender and Law of Polarity are two different laws, and for our purposes, the Law of Gender needs no further explanation. It is the Law of Polarity that shows us how to live peacefully with the opposites.

Because the Law of Polarity IS a law, it is not possible to end war, disease, poverty, lack and pain in the world, for they represent the opposite poles of peace, health, prosperity, abundance and pleasure. We can, however, *personally* experience more peace, health, prosperity and pleasure in our *own* world when we understand how this law operates. We can also use this knowledge to bring order out of chaos.

Also, because of the Law of Polarity, there is no such thing as a "perfect" person. Everyone has both positive and negative traits. Certain people express more of one polarity than the other. And the polarities that some of us consider undesirable are desired by others, and vice versa. For instance, while many American and European women starve themselves in their efforts to be a size 2 or 4, in cities in West Africa, being fat (at least over 200 lbs) represents wealth, health and prosperity, and increases marriage prospects. Women go to extremes to gain weight -- taking dangerous drugs, including steroids, and even eating animal feed.

The Law of Polarity also tells us that every thing and every situation contains both benefits and drawbacks. Remember this when you change your job, consider a business venture, buy a new home, plan a vacation, etc. By being aware of the potential drawbacks in advance, you can make more intelligent choices and prevent some problems altogether.

Don't confuse looking for drawbacks with negative thinking. This is *constructive* thinking, and it allows you to observe what is, prepare for possibilities and challenges, solve the problems you can solve and then let go of the situation or accept it. You don't ignore the negatives in your life -- whether negative circumstances, thoughts or feelings-- anymore than you ignore weeds in your garden. With knowledge, you learn how to handle them. Negative thinking, however, focuses on what's wrong, without seeking a solution, and wastes your time in useless mental states such as worry and blame.

How To Change Polarities

To change the polarity of something you must add its *opposite* energy. For instance, if you want to change something from cold to hot, you add heat. If you want to change something from small to big, you make it bigger (add "bigness"). If you want to change something from slow to fast, you add speed. If you are sick and want to be well, you add healing remedies, treatments, foods and thoughts and images of health, etc.

If you are worried or fearful, you add faith or courage. If you feel anger or hatred, you add love or forgiveness. If you are impatient, you add patience. This is about shifting your attention to the opposite polarity. Of course, it's easier said than done. (And that's why you're reading this book, isn't it?)

You can use the Law of Polarity to clarify and amplify what you want. Sometimes it is only by knowing what is undesired that you become certain of what *is* desired. Also, as you train yourself to see benefits in experiences you don't like, you can learn from them and turn them into blessings. While what you call "bad" still exists, it doesn't cause you to suffer.

The Law of Rhythm

This law reminds us that everything in the universe operates in cycles. There is a pendulum-like movement in all of life. This principle exists in everything on the physical, mental and spiritual planes. Action is followed by inaction, in-breath is followed by out-breath, night follows day, and day follows night again. The great pendulum swings from spring to summer to autumn to winter, and then the cycle begins anew. The tide goes in and the tide goes out.

Shakespeare called it the "tide in men's affairs" and the bible tells us "There is a time for sowing and a time for reaping."

The **Law of Rhythm** helps us understand that energy is not created or destroyed – it goes through cycles. Leaves and flowers bloom, wither and then die, only to be reborn again in another season. Everything in the universe is subject to the Law of Rhythm, including our health, the economy, fashion, philosophies and even our state of mind.

Upswings -- in business, finances, health, efficiency, moods, etc.-- are followed by downswings, and downswings lead to upswings again. As I edit this book, in the summer of 2001, the stock market is in a down cycle, after an exceptionally long up cycle. (It *will* go up again – we're just not sure *when*.)

Our physical energy, mental acuity and emotional states are also all responsive to the Law of Rhythm. These are our personal *bio-rhythms* and explain why sometimes we don't have as much physical energy, are not as mentally sharp and don't feel as enthusiastic as we do at other times. Some of our 'deflated' moods are not related so much to specific events and situations as they are to the rhythms moving within us. Regardless of the reason, unless we stay in a negative mental state, our downswings are sure to be followed by upswings.

How to Be in Harmony With the Law of Rhythm

Animals instinctively recognize the Law of Rhythm. Squirrels save nuts to last through the long winter. Bears go into hibernation. We can take a lesson from our animal friends and provide in advance for downswings (without fear; squirrels aren't afraid as they gather nuts), and we can do *less*, not more, during a down cycle.

While we don't want to go into hibernation (at least not for long) during downswings, these are *not* the times to frantically work harder. If you do, you will give more energy to a situation that is already negative. You need to change your state of mind *first*. The best and quickest way to do that is by practicing GRATITUDE. Start a Gratitude Journal. If you can't think of anything to be grateful for, begin by giving thanks because you can see, hear, speak, move and have a place to live and food to eat. Then continue from there.

While creating faith when it doesn't exist may seem impossible, as does forgiving people you really don't want to forgive, you can use a strictly mental process to begin giving gratitude. Just remind yourself of what you appreciate and how your life is better than some other people's.

Keeping a Gratitude Journal and making entries in it when something good happens in your life (yes, something good happens in *everyone's* life) is a self-nurturing and valuable practice, highly recommended by many personal growth and spiritual teachings. It has even become "mainstream" thanks to the popularity of Oprah Winfrey and the wisdom she imparts on her inspiring daily TV show and in O Magazine.

Chapter 12

THE LAW OF CAUSE AND EFFECT

This law reminds us that everything has a cause and every cause has an effect – whether the causes and effects are apparent to us or not. You turn on the stove to make a pot of coffee, and the heat from the stove causes the water to boil. You watch a commercial on TV and it causes you to buy the product advertised. The product turns out to be shoddy and the effect of that purchase is that you're upset and have the extra work and annoyance of returning it.

In personal growth and spiritual teachings, we call the Law of Cause and Effect *'karma'*, and say, "What comes around goes around," or "You get back what you put out". However, the law has nothing to do with 'punishment'. The Law of Cause and Effect is the operation of *all* the laws of energy, as explained by Hermetic Philosophy and quantum physics. Below is an example in everyday life that illustrates this law.

A young boy goes to bed without dinner, an *effect* that was *caused* by his hitting his little sister, an *effect* that was *caused* by his upset because his father yelled at him, an *effect* that was *caused* by his father being in a bad mood because he had a disappointing day at work, an *effect* that was *caused* by his losing a big client ...and on and on it goes. Where it ends, nobody knows. Nothing happens "by chance"; there is always a cause. It may be very complex or seemingly as simple as being careless or forgetful.

Where Does "God" or the Creator Fit In?

Now, the question comes up: How is the Creator (God, the Source, the Power, Universal Intelligence) related to the laws of energy? I believe that the statement, "It is not for the finite mind to understand the Infinite," is true.

Humans cannot fully know the mystery of the Creator of All-That-Is. However, we *can* understand the laws by which the Creator governs the universe. These are the universal (spiritual) laws, and they are the same as the laws of energy -- the laws you are reading about right now.

Today, we are fortunate to have scientific proof of spiritual principles, yet the world's most esteemed and respected physicists have always been deeply spiritual people. Einstein said, *"Everyone who is seriously involved in the pursuit of science becomes convinced that a Spirit is manifest in the Laws of the Universe."*

Of course, there is much more to know about the universal laws. This book is meant to give you a basic foundation. The Resources section will tell you where you can get more information, including in my Dynamic Self-Healing manuals, which explain the laws in more detail.

Chapter 13

HOW THE HUMAN MIND WORKS

The human mind is a very complex energy system and consists not just of "a mind" but of *three* minds -- a subconscious mind, conscious mind and Superconscious. In addition, there is a non-physical barrier between the conscious and subconscious called the "critical faculty".

Your Conscious Mind

Your conscious mind is the part that is supposed to choose, make decisions and think. Actually, it rarely does this, for what we call "thoughts" are usually *automatic reactions* coming from subconscious programs. Thus, most of our decisions and choices are really based upon our programming. Our programs vibrate, and when we become aware of the vibrations, we call them "thoughts".

The conscious mind possesses a wonderful ability that is rarely used -- FREE WILL. Free will is what makes change possible. With free will we can refuse to be controlled by our undesired programs or influenced by outer circumstances. We use free will when we choose to think thoughts that vibrate in harmony with what we want, instead of allowing ourselves to focus on negativity in our environment or negative thoughts that "pop" into our head.

The conscious mind has very short-term memory. That explains why we must repeat and reinforce anything we want to memorize, any skill we want to develop or any habit we want to create. We must get the information and instructions programmed into our *subconscious*.

Your Subconscious Mind and Its Programs

Your subconscious is the storehouse of everything you have ever seen, heard, tasted, touched, smelled, or in any way experienced. It is the computer-like part of the mind and is full of programs. The programs in your mental computer are like the programs in an electronic computer – they are instructions and directions.

You have programs for every area of your life – physical, mental, spiritual, financial, career, family, social, etc. You have programs about your health, appearance, talents, skills and everything that concerns you and the world in which you live. These programs tell you how to think, feel, function, behave and respond in any given area of your life.

As previously explained, just as electronic computers have operating systems through which the other programs operate, so does your subconscious (your mental computer). Since all other programs must operate through the operating system (the Material Model for most people), it is the *most important* program of all.

Your self-image program, which is different for everyone and determines how you feel about yourself, is next in importance; then come the rest of your programs. Your programs tell you how to respond to circumstances, how to dress, what to eat, what to read, where to go on vacation, who to associate with and so on. They define what's good and what's bad. They "run" you, unless you *consciously* make choices contrary to your programmed responses.

Your primary sources of programming are genetic and environmental. Genetic programming includes everything you inherited by being human, such as the way the parts of your body function and the natural physical changes that occur as you go through each stage of life. It also includes everything you inherited from your parents and ancestors, especially your appearance and natural talents.

Environmental programming is everything you learned -- from your parents, siblings, family, friends, teachers, peers, ministers, television, movies, advertisements, the media, newspapers, etc. -- whether correct or incorrect. It includes your abilities, such as: reading, writing, grooming yourself, communicating, driving, using a computer, performing your job, and everything else you leaned how to do. Genetic and environmental programs both have a tremendous influence upon you, but there is another, largely ignored, very important source of programming – *mass mind. consciousness.*

Mass Mind Consciousness

There is only one energy field, and energy cannot be created or destroyed. Therefore, every vibration -- **every event, thing, thought, belief, idea, emotion and action that ever existed** -- still vibrates in the unified field of energy. We are all connected and are all part of that unified (one) field. We are to the unified field, like a speck of sand is to the beach or a drop of water is to the ocean. Everything that humanity has been vibrating for millenniums is within this field, and these vibrations, collectively, make up mass mind consciousness.

Also called "race mind" and "collective consciousness", Swiss psychiatrist, Dr. Carl Jung, called it the "collective unconscious." He used the term "archetype", to describe unconscious patterns, beliefs and models that are within the collective unconscious, and therefore, part of all of us to some degree. When masses of people believe something for centuries, it pervades the unified field. The vibrations of that belief become part of almost everyone's programming and energy field, and they impact upon our reality.

Never underestimate the power of mass mind consciousness. When masses of people project anger, hatred, fear and other negative vibrations into the unified field, for centuries, mass chaos results. Order comes when masses of people vibrate positive emotions like love, gratitude, appreciation and peace.

The Material Model is a mass consciousness belief, as is the negative programming most people have regarding health and aging. They expect to slow down, become ill, have aches and pains, look haggard and lose mental clarity as they age. Most people also seek drugs or surgery for their health problems, in spite of the fact that medical mistakes kill anywhere from 44,000 to 98,000 hospitalized Americans a year, according to the Associated Press, November 1999.

Many more, who are not hospitalized, die from prescription drugs. (Medical error is the third leading cause of death to Americans, following heart disease and cancer.) While many people use alternative health care occasionally, most still only "believe in" the medical model (an intrinsic part of the Material Model) and use natural therapies as a last resort.

In addition to the mass mind beliefs that affect most of the population, there are beliefs that are common to families, religions, races, organizations, industries, companies, cities, countries and cultures. If we strongly identify with any of these groups, chances are we have taken on their beliefs, often without realizing it. Carolyn Myss, PhD, author of "Anatomy of the Spirit", calls these "tribal beliefs". She also says that if we are going to heal, we must break free from our tribal beliefs (and from the influence of our "tribes").

The Critical Faculty of the Mind

The critical faculty is a "barrier" between the conscious and

Vibrational Harmony

subconscious mind. Its "job" is to prevent anything from reaching your subconscious unless it agrees with what is *already* programmed. This is another reason why change is so difficult. Besides having an operating system that says you are not supposed to change, you have a non-physical barrier in your mind to prevent anything new from penetrating your subconscious.

Fortunately, you *can* break through the barrier and reject what the masses accept, and accept what the masses reject. People with strong intention and passionate desire, who overcome tragedy or go from rags to riches, do this automatically. Hypnosis and certain breathing techniques break through the critical faculty, as does imagery, ritual, movement and sound. Watch sense-stimulating TV commercials and entertainers who perform in front of enormous audiences and observe the sights, sounds, movement, colors and graphic images they use. It's all directed at the subconscious mind.

Besides their powerfully motivating techniques, the media uses *repetition and reinforcement* to get you to respond to their advertising messages. This explains why subliminal tapes that provide continuous repetition and reinforcement for the subconscious can be such effective reprogramming tools. Some of the best on the market are SCWL subliminal tapes produced by Midwest Research of Michigan. (SCWL stands for Subconscious to Conscious Way of Learning, meaning the subconscious learns from the tapes and "teaches" the conscious.) You'll read about them in Chapter 17.

Exciting New Research About the Brain and Mind

Though we consider the subconscious to be like a mental computer, it appears that the subconscious "mind" is really in the body. As doctors and authors, Deepok Chopra MD and Candace Pert PhD, and other researchers now tell us, every thought we think and emotion we feel is recorded in the cells of our body, as well as in our brain; hence, the new term "bodymind". This term tells us that the body and mind are really one and cannot be separated, and gives us greater insight into how mental and emotional stress can result in physical disease. (In reality, your subconscious is not just your mental computer, it is your bodymind computer.)

In "Molecules of Emotion", Pert's 1998 ground-breaking book about the effect of neuropeptides on emotional states, she notes that the neuropeptide chemicals of the brain are programmed by information in the DNA. It appears, then, that some so-called emotional conditions are carried in the DNA of our body cells.

If this is true (and though more research is needed, it seems that it is) current research suggests that some apparently psychological issues are not just "in the mind", as we have believed. This would explain why certain mental or emotional problems are not resolved, in spite of Herculean efforts by both individuals and therapists. It would also explain the remarkable success of energy psychology techniques that work *simultaneously* on the body and the mind.

Consciousness and Programming

The term *consciousness*, in regard to an individual, refers to his or her "programmed" state of mind. A person with a *healing consciousness* is programmed to heal him/herself and/or others. Healing consciousness is what separates health professionals with the same knowledge and training from one another.

Having a *wealth consciousness* means being programmed to attract money and wealth. Donald Trump is a good example. After recovering from bankruptcy, he wrote a book on becoming a billionaire for the second time!

If you sometimes wonder why YOU need to use certain techniques to get what you want, while some people – including people you consider "undeserving" -- get that same thing *without* doing special processes, it's because it is not necessary to program or reprogram oneself for something if one already *has* a consciousness for it.

The mind of a person with a wealth consciousness will always go back to the "default" position of wealth. This is true whether the person is 'good' or 'bad'. If people are *already* programmed for wealth, a miserable personality and unethical behavior won't interfere with their ability to attract money. However, if you're not programmed for money and you want to *change* your programming, these things DO matter because you want to have high vibrations so you can tune into, and get assistance from, your Superconscious.

Chapter 14

THE SUPERCONSCIOUS – YOUR INFALLIBLE GUIDE

Many teachings do not differentiate between the subconscious and Superconscious, but I've always felt this distinction is necessary. Recently, I was pleased to learn that Huna, a powerful ancient spiritual teaching from Hawaii, also makes this distinction. While your subconscious is limited by its programs, your Superconscious -- also called Self, Higher Self, Innate and Higher Mind -- is *unlimited* and connects you to the Power we call God, and to all of Its wisdom.

Your Superconscious can help you get what you want, if you *ask*. You must ask because it respects your free will and never intrudes. To get assistance from this spiritual part of you -- the part that connects you to the Source of all-that-is -- you must ask and also align yourself (i.e: be in *vibrational harmony*) with its high frequency vibrations.

Positive emotions such as love, joy, faith, patience, compassion, forgiveness and gratitude align you with its energy. So does surrender -- that moment when you are devoid of thought or feeling, when you finally "give up and let go" knowing there is nothing more you can do. This explains why people have a spiritual epiphany following their most devastating experiences. In that precious moment they are able to hear the message and are open to Divine guidance. We read about these people, and we wistfully wonder when miracles like theirs will happen to us.

Superconscious Guidance

Intuitive messages come from your Superconscious. How many times have you gotten a feeling that said, *"do this"* or *"don't do this"*, and you regretted later that you didn't listen? We all want to know how to identify whether the inner voice we hear is our Superconscious or our personality (ego) self. Often, especially when you begin spiritual practices, it is difficult to tell, but if you have strong intention and you create a habit of meditating or praying, or if you just sit in silence, you can communicate more easily with this part of yourself and you will begin to recognize its messages.

Your Superconscious speaks to you in a "still, small voice". Cultivating the ability to "tune in" is a skill, like cultivating the ability to paint or play the piano. Some people do this with ease, while others learn how with practice. By having the desire to be open to messages coming from your Superconscious, you will, in time, develop discernment and recognize them. The one thing you can be certain of when something inside of you "speaks to you" is this — your Superconscious never criticizes you, condemns you or calls you unkind names like "stupid". *Never.*

Chapter 15

UNDERSTANDING YOUR FEELINGS AND EMOTIONS

Most people, including me, use the words "feeling" and "emotion" interchangeably, but they're not exactly the same. You can have a feeling, good or bad, without being motivated to *do* anything. Emotion, however, means "energy in motion" (e-motion), and usually leads to strong responses.

While we can learn to master our emotions so we don't take actions we'll regret later or don't suffer needlessly, we never eliminate the ones we classify as negative because, by natural law, everything has its polar opposite, including feelings and emotions. Besides, it's normal, appropriate and human to be fearful when there is danger, to grieve over losses and to be angry at injustice. You cannot change this, nor would you want to. However, you can take action when it's called for and you can decide when to release painful feelings (yes, even those resulting from tragedy) and move on with your life.

What Causes Feelings and Emotions?

Of course, some feelings and emotions are related to traumatic events, but most are caused by our perceptions, thoughts and beliefs. If we don't like something, we get an immediate negative thought and we simultaneously respond with an uncomfortable feeling like fear, anger, resentment, anxiety, sadness, impatience, worry, etc. We welcome our positive feelings, but we often try to suppress negative ones because they feel so bad, or we mistakenly think people involved in personal or spiritual growth should not have negative emotions. DON'T DO IT! As I learned, when my suppressed emotions turned into a critical illness in 1993-94, this can be very dangerous to your health.

Your so-called negative emotions are messengers or "warning signals", telling you that whatever your attention is on -- consciously or unconsciously – is lowering the frequency of your vibrations and is not in harmony with what you want. While these emotions don't feel good, they have a positive purpose. Fear, for instance, is an instinctual response to real and perceived danger that produces specific chemical changes to allow you to flee or fight. This is very necessary when you really are in danger. However, fear is also likely to show up as soon as you decide to take a risk and change something in your life. This is a perceived danger, based on your beliefs.

Feelings Change When You Change Beliefs

People assume that it's impossible to change feelings. That's not true. Though you can't "force" feelings to change (nor should you try), when you change the thought and belief *behind* the feeling, the feeling automatically changes. Your feelings can help you identify your negative thoughts, and these thoughts can lead you to the negative beliefs (programs) that cause the thoughts and feelings. People also assume that anyone in the same situation as they are would feel the same as they do. That's not true either. Something that angers or upsets one person may cause someone else to feel good.

Consider the following examples: Two children try out for the ball team in school and both don't make it. Shellie is pleased she didn't make the team. She tried out because she thought it was the thing to do, but she doesn't like playing ball and is glad she was rejected. Michael is devastated. He's certain his father will be upset and this rejection is a tremendous blow to his self-esteem.

Two husbands call their wives to say they're working late. One wife is angry because she doesn't trust her husband and thinks he might be cheating on her. The other is delighted. Now she can read her great new book. She puts his dinner in the refrigerator and happily takes a long, leisurely bath.

Frank and Jeff both discover their credit card bill wasn't paid on time and now they have an additional $29 late charge. Frank is disgusted and irritated with himself for wasting $29 when money is so short. Jeff shrugs his shoulders as he pays the bill and adds the $29. This is a piddling sum that doesn't mean a thing to him.

Same circumstances, but different emotional responses. Can

you see the differences in these people's thoughts? Their emotional responses were caused by their thoughts of how things "should" (or shouldn't) be, and their thoughts were caused by their *beliefs*. Unless we change (reprogram) beliefs, we're likely to have the same thoughts and, therefore, the same emotional responses to the same or similar situations.

Other Reasons for the Way We Feel

Sometimes negative feelings are caused by the pendulum swing of the Law of Rhythm. Sometimes they are caused by our susceptibility to the vibrations around us. You can enter a room feeling good, but negative conversations you hear around you or the negative vibrations of other people in the room can soon dampen your spirits. Fortunately, the opposite is also true and positive people and environments uplift us.

At highly emotionally-charged events, such as rock concerts or large rallies, participants are very vulnerable to the vibrations in the environment. Sights, sounds and staging of these extravaganzas are designed to put people in mass hypnosis. Should things get out of control, mayhem breaks loose. If some people in the audience become aggressively or sexually stimulated by the sounds, images, movements and activities on stage, the energy field (vibrations) that is created can, and often does, affect other people, including some who usually behave conservatively. While we can't always avoid specific environments and people (and don't necessarily want to), by remaining aware, we can *choose* our responses.

What To Do About Feelings and Emotions

To be human is to have both positive and negative feelings and emotions. Emotions summon energy, so *amplify* your positive emotions; they are powerful magnets for attracting what you want. Now, here's what *not* to do with negative emotions. Never ignore, deny, suppress or repress them, because the negative energy will be stored in your body. That's how you get sick. I did that for years. I wouldn't allow myself to have negative feelings because I "knew" better. (Yes, I knew so well, I almost died.)

Appreciate emotions as the message-bearers they are. Always acknowledge how you feel, whether good or bad. You may choose to experience "negative" (unpleasant or painful) emotions at times, such as anger or grief, but don't stay in that state, as this lowers your vibrations. At an appropriate time, process and release the emotions in order to raise your vibrations and move on with your life.

Keep a balanced perspective so you avoid the letdown feeling that usually follows a tremendous "high". If you get too excited by the things you call "good", the Law of Polarity will ruthlessly show you the drawbacks and the Law of Rhythm will bring you crashing down. Instead of being too infatuated and elated over what you consider so great, feel joy from a serene state and express gratitude for your good fortune.

Regardless of why you feel the way you do, you can prevent

negative emotional energy from getting "stuck" in your body with immediate **action or creativity**. First, take a few deep breaths and then do something creative or physical. Draw, paint, play a musical instrument, beat drums, bang on something, sing or scream, write about your upset (or just write). Or dance, run, race-walk, jump on a trampoline, hit a ball, lift weights, do aerobics, karate, martial arts...whatever exercise you enjoy. You can also use these activities to release some emotional traumas from the past that have become "blocks" in your body. You do this by *saying to yourself*, as you do the activity, "I am now releasing negative energy."

When it's not possible to exercise or do something creative, just do something to **shift your feeling**. Listen to music you enjoy, play with your pet, read something inspiring, watch a funny video -- do what makes you feel good. Let go of the feeling first. Later, you can go back and discover the belief (program) behind the feeling, so you can reprogram it.

Your all-knowing Superconscious will be happy to assist you. Sit or lie quietly, take a few breaths, and ask for beliefs and programs that interfere with you getting what you want to be revealed to you. If you practice this process, you will discover that statements and/or mental images "pop" into your mind. You can identify and reprogram your negative beliefs yourself, using the techniques and energy psychology processes in this book. You may also want help from a professional who is skilled in this field.

Chapter 16

PROGRAMMING THE SUBCONSCIOUS MIND

There is a difference between programming yourself with something for the first time and REprogramming yourself. Programming is much easier.

You can put an infant in a pool and he or she will learn to swim without fear, but you can't do that to a child or adult who already has preconceived ideas (conscious or unconscious) about water, safety and the possibility of drowning. A child can learn several languages at the same time, fluently and with ease. It's harder for most adults to learn a second language when programming related to language is already in the subconscious.

This is because *old programs oppose having new programs installed on the same subject*. (Hmm...sounds just like the way my electronic computer works!) With a true desire to learn, and the willingness to repeat and reinforce the new language (or whatever you want to learn), it becomes second nature. This is how you create a new program -- whether you want to learn another language or become proficient in something you formerly were not able to do well.

Programming and reprogramming your mind – regardless of what you want to put into your subconscious – requires that the new information and messages be *repeated and reinforced* over and over until they are *accepted* by your subconscious as new instructions.

For instance, in order to install the Energy Model so that it replaces the Material Model as your operating system, it is not enough for you to believe consciously that what you are now reading is true. Your *subconscious* must believe it also. This means the new information about energy and the laws of energy (the universal and mental laws) must be repeated and reinforced the way you repeated and reinforced the alphabet and mathematics tables when you were a young child. For that reason I urge you to read, reread and review this material so it is sufficiently reinforced to sink into your subconscious.

I recommend that you read Dynamic Self Healing manuals (see Resources) to give you more knowledge and understanding. And use the techniques in this book to release the Material Model and reprogram yourself to accept the Energy Model as your mental computer's operating system.

When the Energy Model becomes as much a part of your programming and consciousness as the alphabet and mathematics tables, it will be easier to program and reprogram yourself for whatever you desire. With strong intention and a new operating system for your mental/bodymind computer, you can create the life you want.

Chapter 17

THE TECHNOLOGY OF REPROGRAMMING

There are four stages to REprogramming your subconscious mind and only three to programming it. The same stages apply to every area of life.

The four stages are: **Awareness, Releasing, Installing and Integrating.** There are only three stages for programming because, when you program something NEW into your subconscious, and you don't have preconceived ideas to interfere with the installation, releasing is not needed. (You just use the other three stages to program something new.)

The exception is this: if you're programming yourself with something about which you have no similar program, *but* you feel insecure, undeserving, unworthy, guilty, fearful or worried, you need to release the *beliefs* causing these concerns.

For instance, you may not have a program about "dancing" in your subconscious, but if you believe you can't dance, that you're too awkward, have "two left feet" and are afraid you'll look like a fool, etc., those beliefs must be released *before* you can successfully program yourself to dance well.

This chapter gives you an overview of the four reprogramming stages. Details are covered in future chapters.

Awareness

Here's where you become aware of and identify what you want to change in your life – what you want to be, do or have. This might include developing more self-confidence, earning more money, being radiantly healthy, learning to dance, improving your golf game, changing your career, finding a mate, having a better relationship with the mate you now have or with your children or your employer, etc.

Releasing

This is about identifying and letting go of beliefs that are in conflict with what you want (i.e: "I'm not good enough; money is evil; I've always been sickly; I have a poor golf swing, my husband and I don't get along," etc.). Normally, we don't focus on negatives unless we are problem-solving -- in which case we're really focusing on *positive solutions*. However, for the purpose of reprogramming, you *do* focus on negatives because they are blocks that need to be identified in order to be released (or -- in computer language – to be "deleted").

Discovering Different Aspects

When you begin to identify beliefs to release, your mind will bring to the surface different aspects of that belief. For instance, with "My husband and I don't get along", there could be ten things (or is it hundreds?) that you want to reprogram about your relationship. Here are some possible aspects: "We argue over money. We don't agree on disciplining the children. He tries to control me. We have different tastes in entertainment. He doesn't do any repairs on the house. He never compliments me"…and so on.

Now you might ask, and rightly so, "How is my doing processes going to change him?" Well, when the energy field between the two of you shifts because of what you do, he may or may not change, but *your response* to "what is" changes for the better and you feel different. You also have more mental clarity. (Chapter 26 has more information on aspects.)

Installing

In this third stage, you tell your subconscious what you want with intention, affirmations, mental imagery, positive prayer, meditation, etc. Installing (or "downloading" in computer language) includes taking appropriate action. Action is necessary, but usually doesn't work well unless you also deal with the mental and emotional components of the issues.

Integrating

In the fourth stage, you continue to repeat and reinforce everything you do in the previous three stages. When the new programs are integrated into your psyche, your automatic thoughts, feelings, perceptions, attitudes and behaviors are different, for they are coming from new, more positive beliefs. To insure the changes are permanent, continue to reinforce your new programs.

Using SCWL Subliminal Tapes

To help you install and integrate, I recommend SCWL subliminal tapes by Midwest Research of Michigan. These extremely effective reprogramming tools continuously repeat and reinforce thousands of positive messages that are heard only by your subconscious, while your conscious mind hears the gentle sounds of ocean waves or music. You don't even have to actually 'listen' to the tapes. They play quietly in the background while you go about living your life – working, playing, reading, talking, writing, exercising, watching television, etc....anything you normally do.

They work so well because they *bypass* the barrier of your mind (the critical faculty) and go *directly* to your subconscious. I have SCWL subliminal tapes playing all the time. I used two of them constantly when I was critically ill in 1993-94 -- "Psychoneuroimmunology" and "Joy and Happiness". I have no doubt that playing these exceptional tapes is one of the reasons I am alive today.

There are over 130 different tapes (plus 20 CDs) to support change in just about every area of your life. All scripts are positive and approved by a professional peer group and tapes are sold with a money back guarantee. You can read more about them on my website. (See Resources for address.)

Chapter 18

WHY THE SUBCONSCIOUS RESISTS REPROGRAMMING

People involved in self-help and personal growth have been installing new programs in their subconscious (or attempting to) for years. While some people have good results with imaging and/or affirming, many have only moderate success or see no change at all. For some people, things get worse.

One of the major reasons the subconscious mind resists reprogramming is this: The new information and techniques we use are based on the Energy Model, and they are being introduced while we still operate from the Material Model. As long as the old paradigm is in charge, we'll have resistance, because this operating system insists change is difficult, if not impossible, and it does all in its power to make sure we *don't* change. (Fortunately, when you reprogram yourself, your subconscious will work just as hard to prevent your *new* programs from changing.)

Importance of Releasing

Not releasing old negative beliefs from the subconscious is another reason it resists reprogramming. The biblical statement, "You can't put new wine into old bottles", means you can't put new beliefs in a mind filled with old ones. The vital stage of releasing negative programs is neglected because most people never heard of it, don't know any techniques or don't "believe in" it. Unless you know about the Energy Model and are aware of the body-mind energy connection, releasing makes no sense. While it may not be required when programming something into the subconscious for the *first* time, releasing is often the "missing link" in REprogramming.

There is a group of people for whom reprogramming attempts have a detrimental effect. These are people who have been working on themselves for a long time with little or no positive results. For them, popular clichés like, "Do the work you love and success will follow" and "Give service and the money automatically follows," prove to be untrue, no matter how much service they give or how hard they work. As a result, they have lost a lot of self-esteem and confidence.

When they do reprogramming processes – especially repeating affirmations or creating mental images -- they do so fearing they won't succeed (unconsciously, if not consciously) and this becomes a self-fulfilling prophecy. The longer this continues, the more it reinforces their belief that "nothing works" and they "can't change" -- and the worse they feel about themselves and their life.

If you are one of these people, what you are about to learn has the power to transform your life.

Chapter 19

THE "MAGIC" OF ENERGY PSYCHOLOGY

As we learned in Chapter 13, "How the Human Mind Works", Candace Pert PhD, Deepok Chopra MD and other researchers tell us that *every* thought and feeling is recorded in our body. This explains how our mind can make our body sick. (Fortunately, our mind can also make our body well.) When the negative energy of undesired thoughts and emotions get "stuck" in the body, this interferes with the free flow of healing energy, or life force.

Recently, an exciting new field that deals with the body-mind energy connection, called "energy psychology", has emerged. A therapeutic intervention that involves working with the body to heal the mind or working with the mind to heal the body, without drugs, could be considered a form of energy psychology. Innovative techniques to help people with their mental/emotional stresses existed before the term "energy psychology" was used, but many are complex, can only be done with a practitioner and/or take a long time to be effective. The new techniques are simple, fun, work fast...and you can do many of them yourself.

The ones I am particularly enthusiastic about are techniques that RELEASE the energy of negative thoughts and emotions that get "stuck", after they're recorded in the body. These techniques work so well because negative thoughts and emotions are always accompanied by a disruption in the body's "energy system", or "electrical system". By correcting the disruption in the energy system, the mental/emotional distress is also corrected. Sometimes the techniques are so efficient, effective and pain-free, they are barely distinguishable from magic.

The Basis of New Energy Psychology Techniques

According to the ancient teachings of Oriental Medicine and the Tao, there are energy lines (called meridians) and energy points throughout the body. Acupuncturists place tiny needles on meridian points to normalize the flow of energy throughout the body, diminishing energy where it's too strong and increasing it where it's depleted. With many of the new energy psychology techniques, you "tap" on these meridian points while thinking about, imagining and/or saying specific things related to your issues. This simple, yet powerful, process releases the blocked energy.

Though no claims can be made that these techniques heal or prevent illness, the fact is, most illness is caused, partially if not totally, by blocked energy somewhere in the body. When the body's energy or life force (chi, prana) is freely flowing, the body heals, and when the energy is blocked, healing is interfered with. Not only does blocked energy affect the physical body, it is a major factor in other life issues, including self-esteem, lack of success and financial and relationship problems. As amazing as it may seem, these release techniques can improve every area of your life.

A Variety of Techniques

An acknowledged energy psychology pioneer is a clinical psychologist, Roger J. Callahan, PhD. He saw how ancient healing principles could be adapted and applied to modern healing, and he developed **Thought Field Therapy (TFT)**. According to Dr. Callahan, whose findings and theories were first published in 1981, *"The body's little known, but quite well established, energy system is actually the control system for all the negative emotions."* (It seems to me it is also the control system for positive emotions.)

Today, there are many derivatives of TFT and other forms of energy psychology, some of which were developed independently of Dr. Callahan. One of the first doctors to study with Dr. Callahan was a chiropractor, Dr. James V. Dorlacher, author of "Freedom From Fear Forever" and developer of Acu-Power. Surprisingly, the most well-known and widely researched technique based on TFT, called Emotional Freedom Techniques (EFT), was developed by an engineer, Gary Craig.

Other energy psychology techniques include: Tapas

Acupressure Technique (TAT), developed by Tapas Fleming, licensed acupuncturist; Be Set Free Fast (BSFF) by Larry Nims, clinical psychologist; Emotional Freedom and Healing (EM&H) by Richard Ross, personal and transformational coach; Whole Life Healing (WLH) and Positive Energy Therapy (PET) by Stephanie Rothman, certified hypnotherapist; Holographic Repatterning by Chloe Wordsworth, MA and Quantum Therapy by Shoshana Margolin, naturopath and PMD.

These are only some of the techniques. Practitioners are developing their own variations of "tapping" techniques, including using tapping on the meridian points to *install positive* statements as well as to release negatives. This works because the same points can be used for releasing and installing, just as the same acupuncture points are used for increasing or decreasing energy in a patient with a physical illness. (Your body knows whether to release or install.)

An excellent book, describing many energy psychology techniques, including her own, is "Extraordinary Healing", by Marilyn Gordon, Founder and Director of the Center for Hypnotherapy Certification.

Besides Dr. Dorlacher, a number of chiropractors have developed techniques to specifically release negative emotions. Some of these techniques and the doctors who developed them are: Concept-Therapy adjusting technique by the late Thurman Fleet; Total Body Modification (TBM) by

Victor Frank; Neuro Emotional Technique (NET) and Neuro Emotional Anti Sabotage Technique (NEAT) by Scott Walker; Network Chiropractic by Daniel Epstein; Bio-Energetic Synchronization Technique (BEST) by Ted Morter; Body Integration by Rene Espy; Neuro Organizational Technique (NOT) by Carl Ferreri. No doubt there are others, and more will emerge. (Note: while chiropractic always releases blocked energy, these techniques are more specific for releasing blocked *emotional* energy.)

Muscle Testing and Other Energy-Based Therapies

In the 1960s, a chiropractor, Dr. George J. Goodheart Jr., developed a profound muscle testing technique called Applied Kinesiology (AK). By testing a muscle and noting whether it is strong or weak, a tremendous amount of information can be elicited from the body, including discovering allergies and pinpointing weak organs.

Once used only by chiropractors, AK is now an important diagnostic tool for many healing disciplines. When used in conjunction with energy psychology, it can reveal the mental and emotional beliefs and patterns that cause energy blocks. This fascinating and accurate muscle test is possible only because of the body-mind energy connection.

Besides chiropractic, energy-based therapies and body-work techniques that release blocked energy include the following: acupuncture, acupressure, reflexology, Shiatsu, therapeutic massage, Rebirthing, Reiki, Johrei and Pranic Healing. Hypnosis, which is finally gaining the respect it deserves, is an energy psychology technique, as is Neuro-Linguistic-Programming (NLP), which is derived from hypnosis.

The techniques I describe in this book are ones you can do yourself. They can even be taught to children; children love to do them and have great results. If you are serious about releasing blocked energy, I recommend that you also work with a professional, especially in the beginning and particularly if you have very deep issues. While you can do much releasing on your own with the techniques you will soon learn, someone skilled in energy psychology can help you better identify issues, personalize and facilitate the processes and combine his or her energy field with yours, thus adding to the power and effectiveness of the techniques.

Results With Energy Psychology Techniques

I know 'releasing' was instrumental to my recovery from near death in 1994. I read Pat McCallum's book, "Stepping Free from Limiting Patterns With Essence Repatterning," and in addition to whatever else I did, I used Pat's processes (not tapping) plus some of the special chiropractic techniques (TBM, NET and NOT) to release blocked emotional energy. At the time, I did not realize how important these release techniques were. If I did, I would not have stopped using them once I was physically healed. I started using release techniques again in 1999, and now use them constantly.

Aside from my own wonderful personal experiences with energy psychology, thousands of people (my clients among them) are making monumental changes in their lives. After they release the old stuck energy, it is far easier to reprogram themselves for what they want in *all* areas of their lives.

The technique in the next chapter is a version of one I developed in order to teach a non-specific technique at my seminars. Several people told me they used it to lose weight and they found their appetite decreased. Finances improved for a number of people; in fact, a man called to tell me that after he used it for a few days to increase income, he received unexpected money. It has also been effectively used to reduce chronic pain. Some people are so enthusiastic about their results with this simple process, they become clients so they can learn more in-depth techniques, personalized for them.

My clients, most of whom I coach by telephone, enjoy better health, have more self-confidence and a greater sense of self-esteem and worthiness. After doing techniques I personalized for them for a month or so, two clients were able to open their own businesses, others asked for and got sizable salary raises, and several said their marriages were much improved.

Most of all, they all feel good about themselves and their life. Some of these people had spent years in traditional therapy and they still didn't have what they wanted. Now they do.

Chapter 20

BASIC RELEASE PROCESS FOR LETTING GO OF NEGATIVITY

Many teachings, especially spiritual teachings, tell us to let go of negative thoughts and beliefs, but they don't give a technology that tells us *how*. Energy psychology does.

Following is a very easy-to-do, effective "tapping" technique I developed, based on Emotional Freedom Techniques (EFT). You can use it as often as you like, even daily.

This is a non-specific process anyone can use to release negatives, while also installing some positive affirmations. The script is very versatile and can be adapted for many different issues and challenges. Examples of how to do this are shown in later chapters.

The points you are going to tap begin below. Write down and read these points until they are committed to memory. Use two or three fingers for tapping. Tap moderately, not hard.

Point One: Karate Chop point -- the fleshy part of your hand between the end of your little finger and wrist. (The part karate masters use when they break bricks.)

Point Two: at the beginning of each eyebrow and directly above your nose (one finger touching the beginning of each eyebrow and middle finger at the point above your nose that is sometimes called "the third eye")

Point Three: on bone at outer corner of eye (one or both)

Point Four: on top of your cheekbone, about one inch below the center of your eye (one or both sides)

Point Five: indentation **under your nose and above lips**

Point Six: immediately **below prominent "knob" on both collar bones** simultaneously

Point Seven: on the **inside of your wrist** (one or both) Tap with your fingers flat, across entire wrist

Point Eight: on the **top of your head** (the crown)

At each point, you repeat a statement three times, while continually tapping (see next page for statements).

Before you begin, take **three deep breaths** and take **one breath** after tapping on each point. (Breathing in through your nose and out through your mouth is preferable, but is not essential.)

Following are the statements to say at each point:

Vibrational Harmony

Point One: "I now release all programs, patterns, beliefs and judgments that interfere with my being healthy, successful, prosperous and happy."

Point Two: "I love and accept myself and I know that I deserve the best in life."

Point Three: "I release all fear, worry and doubt."

Point Four: "I release all anger, resentment and frustration."

Point Five: "I forgive everyone I have blamed for my problems, challenges and issues, including myself, God and the Universe." (It is important to include the Creator here, using whatever name you prefer.)

Point Six: "I ask for and accept forgiveness from everyone I may have hurt." (Optional -- add "including myself".)

Point Seven: "I fill myself with gratitude, love, joy and appreciation."

Point Eight: "I now vibrate in harmony with, and attract to myself, whatever I need to be healthy, successful, prosperous and happy."

End with a deep breath and say, "Thank you." (You are giving gratitude to yourself, the Creator and/or the universe.)

Note: Forgiveness, as used here, is synonymous with *letting go, canceling or releasing*. It does not mean it's "okay". The main purpose and benefit is for YOU -- it sets *you* free.

You can personalize the process by adding YOUR specific desire to the statements at **Points One** and **Eight**, as below:

Point One: "I now release all programs, patterns, beliefs and judgments that interfere with my being healthy, successful, prosperous, happy **and getting the job I want.**"

Point Eight: "I now vibrate in harmony with, and attract to myself, whatever I need to be healthy, successful, prosperous, happy **and to get the job I want.**"

You can also do this process, leaving out the original words of the process and only stating your desire. Example: "I now release all programs, patterns, beliefs and judgments that interfere **with my getting the job I want.**"

When adapting the process for a specific issue, you can also name the person or thing that your feelings are related to at **Points Three** and **Four**.

Experiment with the process and do it with strong intention. *Concentrate* on what you say and do, and *expect* positive results. You may notice subtle changes, such as tingling sensations, "lightness", a relaxed or happier feeling – or you may notice nothing. Something IS happening…something good.

If you use this simple technique daily you will be amazed at how effective it is. The process "peels away" layers of negative energy from your body, and also helps impress your psyche with your new positive intentions. Think of it as a daily "tune-up" for your energy system.

The points in this process are not the only ones that can be tapped. Some practitioners use less, some use more. Other books may have different points or additional ones. They all work because they all affect your energy system.

When you begin doing release techniques, you may notice that some negative thoughts and feelings become amplified. That's because, by doing the processes, you let yourself know that you're ready to let go of old negative energy. Now your Superconscious will bring to your attention things stored in your subconscious mind that you've forgotten, so you can release them. Welcome intense emotions, for they lead you to look for and discover the beliefs/programs that cause your negative responses. Then you can reprogram them.

I recommend that you drink at least eight to ten glasses of pure water to help the releasing process. Though many people don't do this and still benefit from releasing, it's an important health practice. Your body is about 75% - 85% water, and drinking pure water (coffee, tea and juice don't count) helps you detoxify, whether the toxins are the result of junk food, environmental poisons or negative emotions.

Chapter 21

DIFFERENCES BETWEEN THE MATERIAL AND ENERGY MODELS

You are not trying to "eliminate" the Material Model. You just don't want it running your life any more. Though you are a spiritual being, you are in a physical body and you live in a physical world. Matter, which is composed of dense, heavy, low frequency vibrations, is very "real", but as Aristotle concluded, matter (the physical) *comes out of* the Source, which is non-physical or **meta**-physical (*above* the physical). This non-physical Source is the creative energy of the Universe and it is what you use to create YOUR universe.

What you want is to "delete" the Material Model as the *operating system* of your mental computer (your subconscious mind) and install the Energy Model in its place. In case you need to be reminded why, below are some of the reasons to reprogram yourself so that the Energy Model becomes your new operating system.

*With the **Material Model**, you have no power.

With the **Energy Model**, every cell in your being is alive with the equivalent of a trillion atom bombs – power you can use to create an awesome life for yourself and your loved ones.

*With the **Material Model**, you and the Spiritual realm (the realm of miracles) are separate and rarely meet.

With the **Energy Model**, the realms blend into each other, for there is only one consciousness.

*With the **Material Model**, only weird people have visions, communicate with Spirit guides and ask for and expect Divine intervention.

With the **Energy Model**, Spiritual communication and Divine intervention are normal and natural.

*With the **Material Model**, you are programmed to believe that life is a struggle ("no pain/no gain") and change is difficult -- if it happens at all.

With the **Energy Model**, change is not only possible, it often comes quickly, easily and effortlessly.

*With the **Material Model**, faith must be constantly renewed.

With the **Energy Model**, faith is a way of life.

*With the **Material Model**, chronic diseases are forever. Nothing can heal you; you must "learn to live with it" --

conditions such as arthritis, fibromyalgia, chronic pain, etc.

With the **Energy Model**, your body can heal you, especially if you work with health professionals who understand energy (chiropractors, acupuncturists, energy healers, etc.) and use substances that raise your vibrations (homeopathic remedies, herbs, "live" organic foods, whole food supplements, pure essential oils, etc.).

*With the **Material Model**, certain diseases are almost always fatal (some cancers, AIDS, HIV).

With the **Energy Model**, no disease is impossible to heal.

*With the **Material Model**, God is far removed from you and difficult, if not impossible, to communicate with.

With the **Energy Model**, God is as close as your breath.

Are there enough reasons for you to want the Energy Model to be YOUR operating system?

Of course there are. However, it's not enough for you to believe in the Energy Model and know the laws of energy on a conscious level only; subconscious belief is necessary.

How to Create Subconscious Belief

Repetition and reinforcement is the key to creating

subconscious belief. You learned the alphabet and arithmetic tables by repeating them over and over until they became part of your consciousness. You reinforce your knowledge with every word you read, write and speak and every number you use, add, subtract, multiply or divide. Can you imagine what life would be like if the alphabet and simple math were not committed to memory as part of your programming?

Professor Higgins helped make a lady out of Eliza Doolittle in the marvelous musical, "My Fair Lady", based on George Bernard Shaw's "Pygmalion". With persistent repetition and reinforcement, Eliza's subconscious accepted the "new" person she had become, and everything in her life shifted according to her new beliefs (programming) about herself.

By repeating and reinforcing your knowledge of the Energy Model and the universal and mental laws, this new information will be programmed into your subconscious and accepted as the truth. This gives you a *reason to believe* that the universe is a friendly place, regardless of conditions and outer circumstances. Programmed belief, resulting from repetition and reinforcement, is the kind of "knowing" the bible refers to when it uses the word "faith" and says, "According to your *faith* be it unto you.

With the Energy Model as the operating system of your subconscious (your mental or bodymind computer) you move beyond past limitations, and are open to all kinds of wonderful new possibilities.

Chapter 22

HOW TO REPROGRAM YOUR MIND TO ACCEPT THE ENERGY MODEL

Here's how to release the Material Model and install the Energy Model as your operating system.

Awareness: The first step is to identify these intentions:
1. To release the Material Model and accept the Energy Model as your operating system
2. To accept the belief that everything is energy, you are energy and you can make the changes you want

Releasing: Use the two processes described below. Begin with three breaths and take a breath between each point.

Release Process One: Continuously **tap on Points One through Seven** as you say this statement once at each point: "I now release all programs, patterns, beliefs, concepts, thoughts and feelings that interfere with my accepting the Energy Model as the operating system of my subconscious."

At **Point Eight** (top of head) say "I now attract to myself whatever I need in order to accept the Energy Model as the operating system of my subconscious."

Release Process Two: Continuously **tap on Points One through Seven** and repeat the following statement once at each point: "I now release all programs, patterns, beliefs and emotional traumas that interfere with my knowing that I am an energy being with the power to change my life."

At **Point Eight** say: "I now attract to myself whatever I need, from within and without, in order to know I am an energy being with the power to change my life."

You will be introduced to another tapping release process in Chapter 24 and learn how to adapt that process to further release the Material Model. Because this program has been reinforced in humanity's consciousness for so many centuries, we do several processes. It's wise to repeat them periodically, to prevent the Material Model from taking over by "default".

Installing: Continuously **tap on all Eight Points** while saying the following statement once at each point: "The operating system of my subconscious mind is the Energy Model." Repeat this installation daily for 21 days to create the new mental habit; then repeat periodically.

Integration: Continue to learn and apply the universal laws. They are the 'rules' of the "Game of Life". Can you imagine playing golf or baseball without knowing the rules of those games? It would be pretty hard to win, wouldn't it?

Cultivate the habit of not only reading something inspiring or motivating regularly (you do that, don't you?), but of also reading about the universal and mental laws, the way the mind works, the body-mind energy connection, etc. This is all clearly presented in Dynamic Self-Healing manuals. The more your conscious mind knows and understands, the easier it is for your subconscious mind to accept and believe.

Attend seminars and workshops that enlarge upon the information in this book. In addition to my trainings and programs -- all of which cover the Laws and Vibrational Harmony (regardless of the specific topic) -- I recommend Concept-Therapy, Silva Mind Method and Dr. John F. Demartini's Breakthrough. (See Resources for contact information.) If you're interested in mystical studies, check for Kabbalah classes in your area. This complex ancient Jewish mystical teaching is all about energy, vibrations and spiritual law. The teachings are being presented in simplified formats for lay people. (No, you don't have to be Jewish!)

Since the Energy Model is not yet part of mass mind consciousness, most people will not validate what you are now discovering. It can be difficult to keep your perspective when you have little or no agreement from the outside world; therefore, it's up to *you* to create certainty for yourself. No matter what others believe -- no matter how many people operate out of the old paradigm and no matter what conditions come up in your life -- you hold fast to your truth *– you are an energy being and you have free will.* That means you have the power to change your mind…and your life.

Chapter 23

THE IMPORTANCE OF LOVING YOURSELF

The main reason we don't get what we want, in spite of all our self-work, is because of the operating system that runs our subconscious (our mental/bodymind computer). Another important reason is that we don't love ourselves enough to feel we deserve what we want. Lack of self-love is very prevalent, albeit often unconscious.

You may deny this -- I certainly did -- but when we ask ourselves certain questions, we realize that we don't have enough self-love. Check this out yourself. Do you do things that make you happy? Are you kind to yourself? Do you acknowledge your talents -- or is that too "conceited"? Do you enjoy being in your own company? Do you take good care of your body? Can you say "no" when people impose upon you? Can you make yourself, your needs and your desires a priority, without guilt?

Or is there a voice in your head that often criticizes, condemns or judges you? Do you feel you don't measure up, that you're not good enough? When positive things happen, do you feel unworthy of them? Do you often feel guilty or blame yourself, even for things you know are not your fault? Do you sometimes expect to be punished, even though you're not sure why? Do you get angry at yourself for not being "perfect"?

Most people answer "No" to the first group of questions, and "Yes" to the second group. So let me ask you – is THAT how you feel about and treat someone you love?

The intent of this chapter is to give you food for thought, not explore self-love in depth. There are many books on this all-important subject. I especially recommend ones written by psychotherapist, Nathaniel Brandon, an expert on self-esteem, which is closely related to self-love.

Following this chapter is an energy psychology process for letting go of negative beliefs and feelings about yourself, and then installing positive ones so you can love yourself more (at the subconscious, as well as the conscious, level). Before we get to the process, let me explain why so many people don't feel good about themselves and why self-love is so important.

Why People Don't Love Themselves

The subconscious considers ideas, concepts, judgments and opinions that are repeated over and over to be "the truth". Whatever is repeated and reinforced, especially before the age of five, is accepted and becomes a powerful program (belief) in the subconscious. Most children, and even infants, are judged, criticized, told they are bad and stupid, scolded and punished. This begins with parents (even loving parents), continues with teachers and peers and, depending on the religion, the negative self-image may be confirmed when children learn about "sin". In a home where a parent died or left because of divorce, the child often blames him/herself, thinking, "If I were good enough he/she would have stayed."

Another reason for finding fault with ourselves is the erroneous belief that we should not have negative emotions. When we feel anger, fear or resentment, we believe these feelings are bad and, therefore, *we* are bad. The positive thinking movement, so popular in the 70s, insisted we must always be "up". This is impossible; yet, when we are not up, we believe we have failed.

Dr. Carl Jung's insightful teachings tell us the importance of accepting and embracing our negative emotions, which he called our "shadow self". Loving yourself means loving *all* of yourself, and both emotional polarities are within all humans.

Positive emotions feel wonderful. Negative emotions don't, but they have an important positive purpose. They let us know when we are in danger or when we are giving attention (consciously or unconsciously) to something we don't want. This gives us the opportunity to become aware of what bothers us, choose to handle the situation, change our focus of attention, use release processes — whatever is appropriate for changing our energy and raising our vibrations.

Why Self-Love Is So Important

The emotion that registers the highest vibrational frequency is **love** (closely followed by gratitude and appreciation). The more we feel love, the more we align with the Infinite – the Source of all that we desire. *The ability to feel and radiate love begins with self-love.* The bible tells us to "Love your neighbor as yourself". Good advice and, unfortunately, people are following it. They DO love their neighbors as they love themselves – and destruction, war, murder, robbery, cruelty, rape, abuse, etc., are proof. The human psyche is complex, and one of the fascinating discoveries is that people who hurt others usually suffer at the soul level with self-hatred.

Not quite as bad, perhaps, but certainly not a good thing, is this: People who don't love themselves often sabotage their success. If they attract great wealth because they're in vibrational harmony with wealth for other reasons -- such as entertaining or in some way serving millions of people, for which they receive millions of dollars – they may severely punish themselves, believing they don't deserve good fortune.

We often read about multi-millionaire movie stars, rock stars and athletes who harm themselves with drugs, alcohol, gambling, sexual excesses and abuses of every kind, even to the point of suicide – planned (rocker, Kurt Cobain) or unplanned (comedian, Chris Farley). Though many reasons are given for their exploits in the media, at the deepest level it is usually lack of self-love that causes their bizarre behaviors.

How To Demonstrate Self-Love to Yourself

While you can spend years in therapy because you don't love yourself, you can also feel immediate relief by doing energy psychology processes. The more you do the processes, the more you let go of the beliefs that stop you from loving yourself. In the next chapter, there's a very effective technique for this purpose. Do it with strong intention and enthusiasm Emotion *energizes* your intention and gives it more power! This process will make a big difference in your life.

In addition to doing the process, choose to treat yourself to something special at least every week. You don't have to spend a lot of money -- although you can, of course. You can buy yourself an expensive gift or a lovely inexpensive bouquet of flowers. You can also give yourself the gift of "time" -- time to relax, to read a book for pleasure, to take a leisurely walk, to go to a museum, or to visit people you enjoy being with and don't often see. Consider treating yourself to a massage or other delightful and nurturing self-indulgence. Doing nice things for *you* gives yourself the message that you love yourself...or at least you are beginning to.

Love makes us magnetic and draws our desires to us. We all want to enjoy the magnificence of life. It is normal to want to experience happiness and the wonderful feelings that come from having an open, loving heart. This is not possible without self-love, for to have a love affair with life and truly feel love for others, we must begin by loving ourselves.

Chapter 24

HOW TO CREATE SELF-LOVE

Now that you know the importance of self-love, you should be eager to release the blocks that stop you from fully loving yourself. Let me tell you, from one who suffered a great deal from lack of self-love, when the shift in consciousness comes, it feels exquisite.

This is a two-part process. Part One, which is based on Emotional Freedom Techniques (EFT), releases the negatives, and Part Two installs the positives.

Make a list of what you do not love or like about yourself -- everything you judge, criticize and condemn, every negative belief about yourself, every habit you don't like – so they can be released. It's not necessary to make the list in order to begin the process, however. You'll begin with the "release statements" I will give you.

Meanwhile, start your list and keep noticing what you say to, and about, yourself. If it's negative, put it on the list to release. You don't have to release each thought, judgment or belief as soon as it comes up. You do releases over time. I've found hundreds of negative beliefs, opinions and judgments on myself, and I continually discover more. I love discovering them, so I can let them go.

Releasing - Part One

Tap on the same acupuncture points you learned in Chapter 20 (see below), while making specific statements. Tap moderately, not hard, using two or three fingers.

Point One: Karate Chop point --This is the fleshy part of your hand between the end of your little finger and wrist. (The part of the hand used to break bricks in karate.)

Point Two: at the beginning of each eyebrow and directly above your nose (one finger touching the beginning of each eyebrow and middle finger at the point above your nose that is sometimes called "the third eye").

Point Three: on bone at outer corner of eye (one or both)

Point Four: on top of your cheekbone, about one inch below the center of your eye (one or both sides)

Point Five: indentation **under your nose and above lips**

Point Six: immediately **below prominent "knob" on both collar bones** simultaneously

Point Seven: the **inside of your wrist** (one or both)

Point Eight: on the **top of your head** (the crown)

At each point, repeat a statement while continuously tapping.

Point One (Karate Chop) statement is repeated three times. It always begins with, "Even though", and ends with, "I deeply and profoundly love, forgive and accept myself." The phrase you say in the middle (**you'll see it in bold print**) is repeated as you continually tap on **Points Two -- Eight.** (It is stated seven times, once at each point.)

In case you're wondering, "deeply and profoundly love, forgive and accept myself" is said in order to take care of *psychological reversal*, which is what occurs when the subconscious mind is strongly opposed to the positive changes the individual consciously wants to make.

Statements: I'll give you the statements for your first two release processes, plus an optional release statement. Even if the optional one is not on your list, I recommend releasing it, as it is a common issue. You'll have many other statements on your list, based on your judgments and opinions about yourself. They all go in between, "Even though", and "I deeply and profoundly love, forgive and accept myself."

For releasing, use the words *you hear in your mind*, no matter how unpleasant they are. If your mind says, "I hate myself" or "I can't stand myself", use those words. Those are the words recorded in your subconscious and nervous system.

Begin processes with **three breaths**, say the statements while continually tapping, breathe once between each point and end the process by taking a breath and saying "thank you".

Statements for First Release Process

Point One: "Even though **I judge myself continuously**, I can still deeply and profoundly love, forgive and accept myself."

Points Two -- Eight: "judge myself continuously." (You can leave out the "I" at these points.)

Statements for Second Release Process

Point One: "Even though **I don't really love myself**, I can still deeply and profoundly love, forgive and accept myself." (Yes, you say "love" again.)

Points Two -- Eight: "don't really love myself."

Statements for Optional Release Process

Point One: "Even though **I feel unworthy**, I can still deeply and profoundly love, forgive and accept myself."

Points Two -- Eight: "feel unworthy."

(Note: You do *not* have to "feel" negative feelings; just think and *say* the words. DO put emotion into the *positive* words.)

Variation: Say "release" before the phrase. Examples: **"release, judge myself continuously"**; **"release, don't really love myself"**, etc. Use this variation if you're concerned that you'll reinforce the negatives by repeating them. (You won't, because *your body knows* if you're releasing or installing, but if it reassures you, say "release".)

You can release a number of beliefs and judgments in one session with yourself. If you have a lot of guilt about things you did (or think you did), tap and say, "Even though **I feel guilty about…**" Guilt is dangerous and must be released because it causes you to expect to be punished (on a subconscious level, if not consciously) or to punish yourself.

Adapting This Process to Release the Material Model

Since the Material Model is so much a part of human consciousness, we do several processes to fully release it. Use this one in addition to the one in Chapter 22. Here's how:

Point One: "Even though **I have accepted the Material Model as my operating system**, I can still deeply and profoundly love, forgive and accept myself."

Points Two -- Eight: "accepted the Material Model."

Each time you do a release process, you "peel away layers"

(like layers of an onion) related to that issue. Some issues clear up quickly; others have many layers and take longer.

Installing Self-Loving Affirmations – Part Two

Tap on the same acupuncture points, saying the *same* statement on each point. Your tapping statement begins with, "I love and accept myself unconditionally AND…" That's your "opener". After AND, state the *opposite* of the issue you released. See examples below. Begin the process with three deep breaths and take a breath between each point.

Below are positive statements to install, based on the statements you previously released.

AND I approve of myself
AND I know that I love myself
AND I'm worthy of attracting (fill in whatever you want)

If your mind rejects these statements, say, "AND I **choose to** approve of myself/love myself/feel worthy" OR "I am **beginning to** approve of myself/love myself/feel worthy."

When you do these processes, you are mentally and emotionally "working". You are moving energy. You may need or want extra rest or sleep. I sometimes do an hour or more of processing at a time, but this is not necessary. You can tap out some issues in as little as a minute. Go at your own speed and remember to drink water.

Chapter 25

RELEASING NEGATIVES AS THEY COME UP:

Always acknowledge negative thoughts, judgments, feelings and emotions as they come up, rather than deny, ignore or try to suppress them. Look for their message. Allow the negative energy to motivate you to take positive action, if appropriate. When you're ready -- it could be seconds, minutes, hours or days -- release the negatives.

Before I knew about tapping, I used a breathing technique (see Chapter 28) to release negatives and I devised scripts, based on one in the excellent book, "Feelings Buried Alive Never Die", by Karol K. Truman. These scripts follow.

To release negative feelings and emotions, take a deep breath and with strong intention, say the following, using the specific words that apply to *your* situation and feelings:

"I now release my feelings of (anger, fear, hatred, resentment, frustration, disappointment, anxiety, etc.) about (the situation, event, person that disturbs you) and fill my consciousness with (serenity, calm, understanding, acceptance, gratitude, appreciation, joy, love, etc.). I forgive myself and others wherever needed, and gratefully acknowledge that all is well. Thank you." Breathe. (Optional: before saying "thank you", add — "even if I can't see it right now.")

To release negative thoughts: When you catch yourself saying or thinking something negative about yourself or your life, take a deep breath and with strong intention, say the following, filling in the appropriate words for *your* issue:

"I now release the belief, pattern and/or thought that (I'm stupid; I'm ugly; I'll always be sick; Nothing turns out right for me; I'll never have enough money; People always take advantage of me, etc.). Then say, "I know that's not true, that..." (say an opposite statement).

Examples of opposite statements: "I'm really smart; I'm beautiful/handsome; I'm healing right now; Things turn out great for me; I always have more than enough money; People always treat me with respect, etc.".

End both Scripts with "I forgive myself and others for all incorrect perceptions. I am grateful for the opportunity to become aware of and change erroneous beliefs and thoughts about myself and my life. I know all is well. Thank you."

I still use these quick and easy scripts. Verbalizing opposites with *intention* -- releasing negatives and accepting positives -- is very powerful. However, for aspects of deep issues, I still tap. I also tap when a negative thought doesn't want to leave or an event continues to cause me anxiety. The situation may not change and I may not like it, but my "emotional charge" is gone. Following are directions and examples for using "tapping" to release negatives as they come up.

Point One (Karate Chop) statement always begins with "Even though," and ends with "I can still deeply and profoundly love, forgive and accept myself." **In between, state the feeling and the reason for the feeling, or state the thought or belief.**

First example. At Point One: "Even though **I'm angry because my husband/wife/boss said…** I still deeply and profoundly love, forgive and accept myself."

Points Two -- Eight: "**angry because my husband/wife/boss said…**"

Second example. At Point One: "Even though **I think that no matter what I do, it never works out,** I deeply and profoundly love, forgive and accept myself."

Points Two -- Eight: "**think that no matter what I do, it never works out.**"

Third example. At Point One: "Even though **I feel guilty about (whatever you feel guilty about)** I deeply and profoundly love, forgive and accept myself."

Vibrational Harmony

Points Two--Eight: "feel guilty about (fill in)"

Release thoughts of guilt *as they come up*, no matter how large or insignificant the issue is or was. After you give yourself permission to release guilt, you are likely to become aware of situations about which you still feel guilty, that you have suppressed or long forgotten. (Contrary to popular opinion letting go of guilt will *not* cause you to "sin".)

Releasing negative feelings has nothing to do with whether or not they are "justified". The question is, does holding on to the emotional "charge" and the low frequency vibrations serve you…or *are they causing energy blockages?* If they interfere with you radiating positive vibrations — release them.

In the next chapter you will find out how to reprogram yourself for the specific things you want. There are many examples to guide you.

Remember, before you reprogram anything else, *first* reprogram yourself to accept the Energy Model as your operating system and *second*, reprogram yourself with the Self-Love processes from Chapter 24. This is especially important to reduce the resistance from your subconscious mind. Once these programs are installed, it will be easier to reprogram old beliefs and install new programs. You do not need to do any other processes before doing the Basic Process in Chapter 20, and you can do it as often as you choose.

Chapter 26

REPROGRAMMING FOR HEALTH, MONEY…WHATEVER YOU WANT

Inside of you is the most wondrous computer imaginable. It was programmed before you were born, and it has been programmed and reprogrammed your entire life. Most of the programming was done without your awareness. Now, you are learning how to consciously, deliberately program your bodymind computer (your subconscious) with *your* choices.

You can learn exciting new skills, become more proficient in things you already know, change your habits…whatever you want. However, you must give *new* instructions to this extraordinary computer or it will continue to carry out its old instructions (the programs that have been running your life).

Reprogramming is a continuous process, and challenges are part of life. Without that understanding, the natural ups and downs you experience can cause you to think you are doing something wrong when you may just be witnessing the operation of the Laws of Polarity and Rhythm. If you're sincere and apply what you're now learning, you'll ultimately get what you want. Don't let yourself become discouraged if results are not as quick as you'd like. (Tap on it!)

To reprogram what you want in any area of your life, use the **Four Stages of Reprogramming**, as explained below.

Awareness and Releasing

Awareness: Become aware of and identify what you want. Books and teachers who tell you to "create your intention" or "set your goal" are referring to this stage.

One way to clarify what you want is by **Scripting**. Write down what you want in the form of a script, as if it's a movie, and you are the writer, director, producer and star. Include all areas of life – personal, family, health, mental, emotional, spiritual, financial, career, social, etc. If you want to change your career, describe what you want. If you seek a loving relationship, write down what you're looking for in a mate. Your script will be the basis for releasing, installing and integrating. Refine, change, read and reread it, and when it no longer inspires you, write a new script.

Releasing: Here's where you identify and let go of negative beliefs and emotions that block you from getting what you want. What do you want that you *don't have*? Radiant health? More energy? Plenty of money? Successful career? Loving mate? New car? More time? What interferes with you having these? What DO you have that you *don't want*? Too much work? Clutter? Unpaid bills? Headaches? Fatigue? Smoking habit? Boss you can't stand? Are you holding on to anger, resentment or hostility? These all need to be released.

Vibrational Harmony

We use the processes from Chapters 20 and 24 to release. First, we'll use the process in Chapter 20. Identify your issues; see examples below **in bold print**. If any are yours, use them, along with the ones you've identified.

Here's how to release *what interferes with* what you want: While you continuously **tap on Point One**, say three times, "I now release all programs, patterns, beliefs and judgments that interfere with **(regaining my health, sticking to my exercise program, having lots of energy, having plenty of money, having time to relax, having a loving mate, etc.)**"

Here's what to say to release what *you have and don't want:* "I release all programs, patterns, beliefs and judgments that cause me to **(be overwhelmed with work, live in clutter, not have enough money, have headaches, be tired all the time, continue to smoke, feel angry often, feel hostility towards…etc.)**" Use ONE statement per process.

Continue the entire process, as described in Chapter 20, to **Point Eight** and say, "I now vibrate in harmony with and attract to myself (fill in what you ***want***, relative to what you just released)."

Dealing With Aspects In Releasing

Sometimes you think you have released an issue, only to have it continue or turn up again. This means some aspects of the issue have been released, but there are more. (You don't have to release all of them to have significant results.) Doing the Basic Release Process in Chapter 20 often brings up aspects. When you say, "I now release all programs, patterns, beliefs and judgments that interfere with (whatever you want)", *some* programs, patterns, beliefs, emotions and judgments will be released, and others will be brought to your attention *over time*. Release them as you become aware of them.

You release aspects with the process in Chapter 24. That process can be adapted to almost anything, including physical healing. (Note: these processes do not replace professional health care, as needed.) To use the process, find the words that go in between, "Even though," and "I deeply and profoundly love, forgive and accept myself." The entire statement is repeated three times at **Point One**. Repeat the in-between words (*omitting* the words "I" or "I have") at **Points Two – Eight**. You can also precede these statements with the word "release", as explained in Chapter 24. Examples of aspects follow:

For health issues, think of different aspects that apply to your condition. Here are examples of statements that fit in between, "Even though," and "I deeply and profoundly love, forgive and accept myself:" **"I have a pain in my back; I have poor circulation; I don't eat healthfully; I don't get enough rest; I am under constant stress; I hate taking drugs (or supplements); I am always tired; I feel so unhappy when I am sick, etc."** Of course, you only say what's true for YOU. Do a separate process for each aspect.

If you don't like making sales calls, here's what you might say between, "Even though," and "I deeply and profoundly love, forgive and accept myself:" **"I don't want to make sales calls; I can't stand rejection; people are rude to me; I don't feel confident; I can't stand it when I don't make a sale and waste my time; I feel I have to struggle for the sale; I hate when people give me the runaround; I feel intimidated when prospects ask too many questions."**

Remember to breathe and drink water when releasing. As you uncover aspects, you're getting deeper into your issue. This can cause you to feel terrific or feel uncomfortable. (See Chapter 29, The Challenge of Reprogramming)

Installing

Affirmations: These are powerful because they project sound vibrations, as well as your thought vibrations. Make sure your affirmations are positive. (Only use negatives for *release* statements.) You can use other people's affirmations as guides, but it's important to create your own. Begin affirmations with **"I am"** (healthy, happy, rich, successful, loving, confident, etc.) UNLESS your mind says, "Who are you kidding?". In that case, say, **"I am becoming"** or **"I choose to…"** instead. Soon it will feel natural to say, "I am".

Your script contains many affirmations. Choose some from the script to say daily, preferably aloud ("mouth" the words or say them silently, when that's not possible). Always focus on their meaning and create a positive *feeling*, as if what you affirm is *now* in your life. Emotions *energize* your affirmations, so say them with passion and enthusiasm. When they no longer inspire you, create new ones, just as you create or alter your script. Say positive statements anytime, as often as you like, related to the issues you release. When you catch yourself thinking or saying something negative, reverse the thought or statement. Do this by saying, "That's not true", and follow with a positive statement. Also, throughout your day, use *statements of intention*. For instance, before driving, think and say (aloud or to yourself), "I get to (destination) safely and easily." Before making a business call, say, "This call is successful and…" (add whatever result you want).

Mental Imagery and Visualization: To mentally image or visualize means to *imagine* whatever you want in your life. Most people use the two terms interchangeably, but there is a difference. When you visualize, you mentally "see", while when you image, you can use any sense(s); "sight" may or may not be one of them. If you're not a visual person, just get a *sense*, a concept, a feeling, of what you want to create.

If you can imagine or visualize your home or a vacation trip you've taken, or what it feels like to be in the arms of your romantic partner (present or past), you can visualize or imagine whatever you want to bring into your life. Try this -- imagine going to your refrigerator, taking out a lemon, cutting it and sucking on it. If you really put yourself into the scenario, you'll find that you actually begin to salivate.

If you want lavish abundance and wealth, imagine money flowing to you from all directions, and imagine the joy you'd feel if you were wealthy, surrounded by money and luxury. Imagine yourself healthy, successful, in a loving relationship – whatever you want. What would that *look* like to you? What would it *feel* like? What would you be *doing*? What would you be *wearing*? What *words* would you be *hearing*? *Who* would be with you? This is what you create and imagine in your mind. Spend a few moments totally engrossed in your images (how long is up to you – anywhere from one minute to ten or more). Then, throughout your day, "pop" these images, feelings or thoughts into your mind for 20 seconds or so.

Tapping: Tapping was originally used only for releasing, which is what it still is most commonly used for. However, as you learned, we also use it for installing. You can give some affirmations more "power" by repeating them as you tap on one or more acupuncture points (say the same affirmation once at each point). You can also tap as you create your mental images (unless this distracts you from your images). Tapping is so versatile that you will probably think of new ways to use it. I even use tapping to memorize words of new songs prior to doing cabaret shows. It works great!

Mediation and Prayer: Spiritual practices are excellent for installing. First, do your practice, *as you normally do*. At the end of your meditation, *focus* on your desires and goals. In prayer, say (and "feel") positive statements regarding what you want, and include gratitude. New Thought religions use positive prayer for healing everything -- all conditions of life -- in addition to physical health. Science of Mind treatments and Unity affirmations are both forms of positive prayer. Many people who pray and/or meditate do not focus on what they want, thinking it's unspiritual. This is not true. After all, the bible tells us (paraphrased) that it is "the Father's good pleasure to give us the Kingdom." But you must ask! By imaging what you want and making positive, grateful statements while praying or meditating -- such as, *"I am grateful for my vibrant health"; "Thank you for the money that is flowing to me"* -- you are asking.

Action

Action steps – what to *do* about almost anything — is well covered in many excellent self-help books, tapes and seminars. Some situations or life experiences won't change until you take action, no matter how persistent you are with mental processes. Even if you could create by just imaging and affirming, your mind probably wouldn't believe it, so it wouldn't work. On the other hand, taking action, without having corresponding programs in your subconscious, will rarely be continued long enough for you to have results.

Many people try to image themselves thin without changing their behaviors, and they fail. Of course, many people don't lose weight even though they diet and exercise. They don't do the mental work, so their mind believes they're "supposed" to be fat, no matter what they do. Not changing programming explains why New Year's resolutions usually last less than a week. You need to do both: take action and reprogram your mind. This applies to anything you want to change or create. It's important to believe that you *can* make the changes you desire. If you consciously or subconsciously think, "It won't work" (whatever "it" is), it won't -- no matter what you do. Use tapping to release the thought, beginning with, "Even though I believe (name your "it") won't work…"

One of the best ways to determine your action steps is to decide what you want to change, and then **ask yourself questions.** These questions should be "action-oriented", such as: What do I need to *do* in order to increase my self-confidence? To improve my health? To lose weight and keep it off? To find the right man/woman for me? To have better relationships with my children? To be more effective in my business? To attract more customers? To find the right job? Ask questions about anything you want to improve or change. Sometimes the answer will be that you need more information. If so, be sure to get it.

Getting knowledge and acquiring skills are forms of action. For instance, if you want to be a professional pianist, you will first have to learn to play the piano. If you want to be a graphic designer, you will have to study art, design and computer graphics. If you want to manage your investment portfolio, you'll need to learn about money management and investment options. If you are newly single and want a social life, you'll want to find out where to meet other singles, etc.

If you have a health challenge and are interested in natural healing, you'll want information on alternative therapies, nutrition, fitness, etc. Also, begin taking simple immediate actions such as exercising, improving your nutrition, getting more rest, working with a new health professional, etc. Unfortunately, health is probably the most confusing subject there is, besides personal growth. That's why I wrote Dynamic Self-Healing manuals when I regained my health, after nearly dying. The manuals give you solid information in simple, clear language and an easy-to-follow format that removes confusion and tells you how to regain and maintain health on all levels -- physical, mental, emotional and spiritual.

If you want a romantic partner, tell the universe this is a priority by making a list of what you want in that person. Then go to places and do things where you can expect to meet someone who has the qualities you value. Most important, to attract love, you must *be* loving and love yourself. Then you can attract a loving partner.

If you want more money and/or a change of career or business, know what you love to do and find a way to make your products or services so desirable that people will gladly pay you for them. While specific action steps for business success is not within the scope of this book, there are countless books, manuals and trainings to help you, including government sponsored programs. Be sure to release any beliefs that interfere with you being successful.

Chapter 27

INTEGRATING NEW PROGRAMMING INTO YOUR DAILY LIFE

Repetition automatically integrates your new programs, until they become as much a part of your life as your current ones are now, and eventually replace those you don't want. Continue reinforcing them by being conscious and aware, monitoring your thoughts and feelings, using the processes and *focusing* – through imagery, thoughts and words -- on what you *want* (not what you don't want). While we can't control all the thoughts that "flit" through our mind, we can choose what we give our attention to.

To reinforce better **health**, *remind yourself* throughout the day that your body is self-healing, that you are taking care of yourself -- making sure that you do -- and that health is normal and natural. If negative thoughts and feelings surface, use the processes in this book to release them.

To reinforce **money** (wealth, prosperity) bring yourself into vibrational harmony with it. Visit stores that sell expensive designer clothes, furnishings and luxuries. Look at magazines that exude wealth, prosperity and beauty and tell yourself that what you see will soon be yours (instead of moaning because you don't have them). Keep your vibrations positive as you pay your bills, by doing something that makes you feel good (like listen to music). If you're jealous or envious of wealthy people, especially those you don't think deserve wealth, tap on the negative thoughts and feelings. Be in a *positive* state of mind whenever you're dealing with, talking about or thinking about money, so you don't repel it.

Here's a simple, yet powerful, mental trick: Carry a $100 bill with you and mentally buy everything you can with one hundred dollars. (Mentally spend the money over and over again.) You can also carry several $100 bills to "spend".

If you want more **self-confidence**, remind yourself often that you are competent. Congratulate yourself when you do something well, even if it's a little thing. If there are areas of your life in which you need more skills in order to feel confident, then get the skills…or give up the need to excel in those areas. Only you can decide which to do.

Be careful that you don't reinforce negatives in speech, either when talking to yourself or to others. People love to commiserate with each other about all the bad things in life (theirs and other people's), but that just puts you in vibrational harmony with those negatives. Listen to your own **self-talk**. When it's negative, don't get angry with yourself. Instead, be thankful that you noticed, and then make a reverse statement. For instance, if you tell yourself, "How stupid I am; I always make mistakes." (Hmm…sound familiar?) you then say something like this: "That's not true; I'm intelligent and it's okay if I sometimes make a mistake."

And, of course, continue to feed your mind with information that will increase your faith, confidence and belief that you can be, do and have whatever you want. Ralph Waldo Emerson was a New Thought philosopher who said (paraphrased) that there is no such thing as having a desire without also having the ability to fulfill it. That means you are *meant* to be, do and have what you truly desire.

A Paradox of the Mind

What we *want* is chosen by the conscious mind, but what we *get* is determined by the subconscious mind. Yet, success trainings tell us that we get what we focus our attention upon. That would suggest that we 'should' get what the conscious mind wants, since that's what we are presumably focused on.

The truth is, we rarely choose our focus of attention. By not *consciously* choosing our thoughts, we allow our subconscious to decide what we will focus upon, and it automatically 'chooses' something that fits in with our programming — whether or not we actually want it. That's why it's so important to make a conscious choice to focus on what you want. As you do that, and also *reprogram* your subconscious mind, your conscious and subconscious will be aligned, both 'wanting' the same thing. **Then** you get what you want!

Chapter 28

THE HEALING POWER OF YOUR BREATH

We all know the importance of air. We can live for days without food and hours without water, but only for a few minutes without air. We breathe about 15 times a minute; in a normal breath we take in and give out about one pint of air. By breathing deeply, we can take in an additional three pints. According to eastern masters and some western physicians, we can balance our nervous system, strengthen our immune system and heal much of what ails us with our breath.

When you breathe, you not only take in oxygen, you take in the essence of life. The Chinese call it "chi", eastern Indians call it "prana" and westerners call it life force. If you seek enhanced health, less tension, more vitality and peace of mind, you can begin with simple breathing exercises.

Letting Go of Stress

Dr. Andrew Weil presents this breathing exercise in his books and seminars. It's simple, yet very powerful and beneficial. Breathe in for 4 counts, hold for 7, and breathe out for 8 counts. Dr Weil recommends doing four cycles of this breath twice a day, but you can do it as often as you like.

As you do breathing exercises, put your tongue on the soft palate in the center of your mouth, between your upper teeth and the roof of your mouth. This is "the centering button", and according to yoga philosophy, holding your tongue on that spot during breathing exercises prevents loss of energy.

Releasing Through Your Breath

Before I knew about tapping, I learned ways of releasing through the breath. I did not realize the value of these breathing exercises at the time. Here's one to use when you are in the midst of emotional upset. You can tap later, especially on the various aspects of the problem, but this breath can take the "edge" off the trauma immediately.

Breathe in through your nose, while visualizing violet light entering your body through the crown of your head. Hold. Breathe out through your mouth and visualize the energy leaving, while thinking, "I am now letting go of (anxiety, fear, frustration, etc., about…). Your issue follows "about".

Use rhythmic breaths -- count 4 (or 6) for the in-breath, hold for 2 (or 3) counts, breath out to the count of 4 (or 6). Repeat 3 times or more. Do this breath as needed, to calm yourself. You can also do this breath anytime for as long as you want. It has many wonderful benefits, including assisting you in your spiritual development and evolution.

Chapter 29

THE CHALLENGE OF REPROGRAMMING

If reprogramming sounds like a lot of "work" to you, let's consider *why* you do it. When you have a programmed belief, it creates a *blind spot* (called "scotoma") on a subject or issue. This makes it impossible for you to change your opinion on that subject or issue, *even if you want to*. (Religious, racial, weight and gender prejudices are all examples of scotomas.)

Your beliefs determine your thoughts, feelings and behaviors. Every thought you think, word you speak and feeling you have vibrates. Most so-called thoughts that "pop" into your conscious mind are really *automatic responses* coming from your programming. They vibrate from *your* energy field into the *unified* energy field, and attract to you the people, things, conditions, circumstances and events that you're in vibrational harmony with. These become your life!

Unless you can monitor and change every single negative thought, perception, feeling and word (an impossible job), you want to reprogram yourself, because negative vibrations are "magnets" for negativity -- such as illness, accidents, chaos, difficult people, financial problems, etc. When your subconscious is reprogrammed, your vibrations (from your automatic responses, thoughts, feelings, behaviors, etc.) come from your positive *new* programs. Now you can resonate with what you want. THAT'S why you go through the "work".

Understanding Subconscious Resistance

There are a number of reasons why the subconscious resists reprogramming. First, the new programs come up against the Material Model, the "operating system" of your mental/bodymind computer, and that program says *you can't change*.

Second, the critical faculty, the barrier between the conscious and subconscious, has the job of making sure nothing penetrates the subconscious unless it agrees with what is *already* programmed. Third, programs are not just in "the mind"; they're recorded in the *nervous system and cells of the body* and it takes time to change the energy-matter of the body. Fourth, most people are trying to put new programs into a container (the subconscious) that's already full. They don't know about *releasing* -- and unless they understand the body-mind energy connection, releasing doesn't make sense.

Some programs represent deeply entrenched habits and a lifetime of conditioning. Also, when unplanned and unanticipated changes occur, we automatically resist the ones we don't like. Not only do we have to reprogram ourselves for what we want, we also have to reprogram ourselves to deal with the changes we *don't* want.

Years ago, I learned the TEA formula from Concept-Therapy. TEA stands for Transmute (change), Eliminate or Adapt. When something disturbs us we must change it, get it out of our lives or learn to live with it peacefully. If we can't eliminate what we don't like, we either change the "thing" itself, or we change our *attitude* towards it. (Changing our attitude is what allows us to live with it peacefully.) Whichever you decide to do involves reprogramming. Fortunately, almost anything can be reprogrammed if the intention is strong enough, because we now have the information, tools and techniques we need.

Programming yourself with something *new*, such as new skills, is less work, because you don't have resistance from old similar programs (unless you are programmed with: "I can't learn…" or "I don't have confidence in my ability to…").

Importance of Your Conscious Belief

If you believe something at the subconscious level, it manifests in your life and does not need reprogramming (unless you want to eliminate it, of course). Until you are programmed with what you want, your greatest ally in dealing with the challenge of reprogramming is your *conscious* belief. If you are not programmed (i.e: don't have the subconscious belief) for health and/or wealth, for example, you will not be "inclined" to think thoughts and take actions that are likely to produce greater health and/or wealth. That's because your *subconscious* wants you to stay exactly as you are.

Therefore, your *conscious* belief that you can change your programming and become healthy and wealthy, regardless of your current circumstances, is essential to reprogramming yourself. Your conscious belief leads you to use your *free will* and make choices that are in opposition to the automatic responses coming from your subconscious. Conscious belief is the result of *knowledge* – of knowing and understanding "how life works" (the Energy Model, the universal and mental laws, vibrational harmony, etc.) It is your conscious belief that motivates you to *persist* until you succeed…in spite of subconscious resistance and challenging outer conditions.

Why We Need So Much Repetition

Everything we want to learn or remember must be programmed into the subconscious mind, which learns by repetition and reinforcement. Some people resist the idea of repeatedly affirming and imaging what they want, saying that God doesn't need to be told what we want over and over. That may be true, but we are not trying to convince God; we're convincing *ourselves*, especially our subconscious.

The power we call God expresses through us according to our beliefs -- and beliefs and programs are the same thing. Your subconscious operates like a computer, and is programmed with the instructions for your life. These are the "default" settings. By repeating and reinforcing the new programs you create, you prevent your subconscious from going back to default, and ultimately, you become "reprogrammed". Of course, we can and do override negative default settings by using will power, but we can't do this continuously – which is why reprogramming is so important. (See Dynamic Self-Healing Manuals for more information.)

Benefits of Reprogramming

Most people immediately feel good as they release the blocked energy of limiting beliefs and "stuck" emotions. When you do processes, you may yawn, feel tingling sensations or feel subtle energy shifts within you – especially during and after releasing. You may feel "lighter" as a result of "peeling away" layers of negative energy. When you install the positive new beliefs, you feel (and you *are*) empowered!

A great bonus of reprogramming is that besides changing the issues you're working on, other issues often improve or disappear. In addition, as you release negatives in certain areas of your life, other negatives are released and you gain clarity in more areas. It's as if you're sweeping out cobwebs in your brain. Personally, my mind is much sharper, my singing is better, and I can work less and accomplish more.

How Your Subconscious May Respond

Reprogramming processes are safe and gentle, but no one can predict how anyone will respond or how long something takes to change, anymore than we know how long it takes someone to learn a foreign language or learn how to drive.

Sometimes the subconscious "fights back" because it doesn't want to change. This can cause uncomfortable reactions. You may cry or have a headache or stomachache or you may feel fatigue, anxiety or irritation. These are all *good* signs and usually pass quickly. (If you have no reactions, it doesn't mean you're not having results; results are inevitable.) The processes may stir up old, long forgotten memories and emotions that have been stored as negative energy. They are coming to your awareness so you can let them go.

If you ever feel overwhelmed, you can do less releasing. As you reprogram yourself, changes also take place in your nervous system and the cells of your body. These are positive changes, for you are improving the "circuitry" of your body's electrical system and increasing the free flow of life force.

How To Enhance Reprogramming

Working with professionals who use energy psychology techniques is very valuable. Besides energy psychologists, some psychotherapists, hypnotherapists, NLP practitioners and other health professionals now use them. Also, I recommend working with practitioners who *physically* move energy. I get regular chiropractic care. Other effective healing systems based on the body-mind energy connection include acupuncture, acupressure, massage and reflexology, and there are others. Knowledgeable professionals can assist and reassure you as you go through mental, emotional, physical, and even spiritual changes.

Be sure to call upon your Superconscious for help. This unlimited, all-knowing, Infinite part of you awaits your request. It never intrudes, for it honors your free will. However, if you ask, you can have profound guidance. Hold a strong intention for what you want. Give a prayer of gratitude, request assistance in identifying the issues to be released and ask to be able to reprogram yourself with ease.

What Can Be Programmed and Reprogrammed

The possibilities are endless. You can program or reprogram yourself for whatever you want and are willing to work for -- more success, health, money, better relationships, a new career, etc. You can create new programs for almost any talent or skill you want. (Know that if you desire something strongly, the means to have it are within you.)

You can also program yourself with any quality or attribute -- compassion, gratitude, appreciation, patience, etc., by adapting the process in Chapter 31. To gain more patience and/or compassion, you are likely to attract people who "try" your patience or compassion. This may be uncomfortable, but it is what helps you develop the qualities you want.

I reprogrammed myself from being so sick I nearly died to being vibrantly health. Recently, I reprogrammed myself from a time-pressured "workaholic" to a person who joyfully takes time for myself. I also reprogrammed myself to exercise daily and love it. This is a 'miracle', as I used to dislike it intensely.

Chapter 30

FAITH, CONFIDENCE AND BELIEF

A brilliant mentor and friend of mine, the late James W. Parker, DC, founder of the Parker Chiropractic College in Dallas, Texas, coined the term "FCB". It stands for Faith, Confidence and Belief.

FCB is the state of mind that allows you to be, do and have what you want. Every success teaching -- philosophical, psychological, religious or spiritual – tells us that faith (or belief) is essential for growth, healing and abundance. The most popular book in the world, the bible, says: "As a man thinketh in his heart, so is he." (Thinketh in his heart means *believe* or *have faith in*.)

We are told to pray, *believing*, and the prayer will be answered. Believe in *yourself*, in what you want to do or be, and in the Power that created the universe. When we read about the hardships famous successful people endured before they got their big break, we know that it is the power of their belief that kept them from being discouraged and quitting. People who recover from terminal illnesses often say they healed because of their faith in God; others claim they had faith that their doctor would save their life. Still others heal because they have faith that the body is a self-healing organism and if they do certain things and take certain substances, they'll get well.

When I was critically ill, I was in the last category. I did not believe in myself or in any doctor's ability to save my life. I was sustained by my belief that my body would heal if I did the right things, and I believed that what I was doing was "right". (I guess it was, because I'm still here!)

True faith is accompanied by action. With faith, we are guided to take the right action steps for us. When we have faith that our health will be restored, we "coincidentally" meet someone who knows the right health professional for us. When we believe we can get a better job, we prepare a resume and go on interviews. If we believe we are ready for a romantic relationship, we go where single people with the same interests as ours are likely to be. Having faith does not mean that we sit and wait for God or the universe to bring us what we want, like the genie in a magic lamp. Rather, we enthusiastically take steps to help make it happen.

The problem with faith is that if you don't have it, you just don't have it. It makes no difference how many times someone tells you to "have faith", it doesn't happen until (and unless) it happens. Sometimes faith comes spontaneously after one survives a life-altering trauma. Though it is unlikely to appear on demand, you will soon learn how to "create" faith, even when you don't feel it.

How Important Is Confidence?

Most success trainings tell us we can't achieve what we want without self-confidence. Nevertheless, some people become extremely successful, though they have little confidence. In fact, there are many stories of famous actors who grow up in show-business families feeling unloved, unattractive and unsure of themselves. Following are two examples:

In a Vanity Fair interview in 2000, Jennifer Aniston revealed the agonizing insecurity she felt as a child and teen-ager, who was constantly criticized by her perfectionist mother. Yet, she became a beloved television star (and a very young multi-millionare), thanks to her role on the television hit, "Friends". Not only that, she married Brad Pitt, a movie star idol.

Jane Fonda told Oprah in the November, 2000 issue of O magazine, that she didn't "find her voice" until she was 62 years old. Her childhood and young adulthood were so painful that she was bulimic until age 32. Still, Jane won two Academy Awards, became a fitness guru and married one of the richest men in America. If confidence is so important, how can we explain these successes, and the success of other entertainers and celebrities who claim that when they began their careers, they were anything but confident?

Though we can't know for sure, my guess is that being born into a show business family is a major factor. Their childhood *conditioning* and inherited talent made show business "a natural" for them. People who didn't have this kind of conditioning need to *create* confidence and belief in themselves and their ability, in order to have the motivation and persistence to go after what they want.

What About Fear?

Confidence does not mean the 'absence' of fear. In their book, "Mastering the Impossible", Siegfried and Roy, extraordinary illusionists and magicians, reveal how they sometimes trembled with fear before performing a new illusion for the first time. When dancer Joyce Jamison received rave reviews on opening night after dancing the magnificent ballet, "Cry", she was afraid that she could not go through the exhausting dance again. There are stories of actors whose stage fright is so severe, they must almost be pushed on stage.

People who know they have prepared themselves well are able to do what they need to do even when they are fearful. Since the heightened body responses (the adrenalin "rush") caused by fear are the same as those caused by excitement and enthusiasm, they use this energy to propel themselves to greater accomplishments...*in spite of* their fears.

Fear is negative faith and has strong attraction power -- it attracts more negativity, including what you most fear. The exception is when you transcend your fear, as above, and instead of being traumatized, you take inspired action.

Why Faith Is So Important

When you know what you want and you focus on it, and energize your desire with the strong emotion of faith, you attract what you need to get what you want. (Conversely, when you focus on what you want with fear, you repel it, for you are really focused on the *lack* of what you want, and so you attract more "lack"… or more of what you fear.)

The faith I refer to is *programmed* faith -- absolute "knowledge" about something at the inner level. The days of expecting people to have "blind faith", based on someone's interpretation of God's words, are over. In today's scientific and high tech world, faith, for many people, comes from knowledge and understanding. Sometimes people are not even consciously aware of their level of faith; yet if faith is programmed into their subconscious, it creates a powerful *electro-magnetic* energy field. As a result, they attract the "right" people, things, conditions, situations and circumstances.

Here are more reasons why faith is so important: True faith and subconscious programming is really the same thing, and, as we know, we get what we're programmed for. Faith, like unconditional love, puts us in resonance with our Superconscious and connects us to the Infinite. When we ask for something, *knowing* it is coming to us, that Power graciously bestows Its blessings upon us. Of course, many people feel they "have faith" and still don't get what they want. The question is, "Why"?

Vibrational Harmony

Why It Can Take So Long to Get What We Want

I have often pondered this, so let me share some thoughts with you. When we ask for something, we may not be ready for it; that is, the timing may not be right. During their interviews, many popular entertainers claim they "knew" from childhood they would be a star. For instance, country singer LeAnn Rimes watched performers on TV when she was two and three years old and said, "That's what I'm going to do". Was she 'supposed' to become an immediate star? LeAnn was on the Star Search TV show and didn't win. Most Star Search winners have long been forgotten, but at the right time, LeAnn emerged as a country music superstar.

Actress-singer, Ann Margret, came to the United States as a young child and when she saw the marquee of Radio City Music Hall, she told her parents she would be performing at that grand theater. Years later, her movie, "Bye, Bye Birdie", opened there, and years after that, she performed, live, in Radio City Music Hall. Yes, it took years. Maybe the bigger the dream, the more time it needs to manifest.

There are many 'rags to riches' stories about people who once lived in their cars, who were down to their last dime, who had no idea where their next meal was coming from. They all said their faith sustained them. Sometimes not getting what we want is a blessing. Many celebrities are showered with success and get too much too soon, and they suffer much tragedy because they're not ready for such wealth and power.

Perhaps certain life experiences are necessary before we can get what we want. Perhaps what we want, and have faith in, is conflicting with a greater vision we are not even aware of. Many people have said they thought they wanted something with all their heart and soul and could not understand why it was withheld from them, until something far more magnificent came into their lives.

Perhaps vibrations of faith are being neutralized by negative vibrations from old fear-based programs. Or perhaps there are unrecognized feelings of unworthiness, guilt or doubt that are also vibrating and need to be released, before you can attract what you want.

If you have a dream and it's not happening *yet*, I urge you to "keep the faith" and reinforce your faith any way you can.

Why Prayer Is So Powerful and How Placebos Work

Inherent in the human psyche is the need to believe, and to have something to believe *in*. Primitive man had his statues, idols, gods and magical objects. Even in this scientific era, people rub lucky charms, rabbit's feet, horseshoes, magic coins and anything else they consider lucky.

Doctors give patients placebos – harmless non-medicinal pills and powders – and tell them how remarkable their new "drug" is. Does this work? Yes, so often it defies logic and reason. To me, since I know the laws and the power of the human mind, it is perfectly logical. These innocuous objects and potions give us faith, and faith is the magic ingredient. The danger is that if something happens to the placebo, something also happens to our faith. It is much better to have faith based on knowledge and understanding.

Prayer is another story. We are told that when we pray *believing*, our prayers are answered. Prayer is also based on faith, faith in the Source of All-That-Is. While just one person praying makes a difference, consider the effects of many people praying. When several or dozens or hundreds or thousands pray, all believing in a Power that can do anything, it creates powerful high frequency vibrations (energy fields) that impact upon the unified energy field that makes up our universe. Results are often astonishing, as described by Larry Dossey, MD, author of "Prayer is Good Medicine".

In August 2001, network television had a segment on prayer, which included an interview with Dr. Deepok Chopra. In spite of the marvelous benefits and healings verified on the show by doctors and people who did not know they were being prayed for, traditional scientists remained unconvinced. Yet, if a money-making drug was as effective as prayer, it would be hailed as the drug of the century.

Fortunately, when faith is lacking, if one wants it enough, it *can* be created. The process in the next chapter tells you how.

Chapter 31

HOW TO CREATE FAITH

You create faith the same way you create anything else you want – you *program* it into your subconscious mind, using the reprogramming processes. **Identify** what you want to have more faith *in*. Use the processes to **release** beliefs that interfere with your faith. **Install** affirmations and images of faith. **Integrate** by reinforcing your faith, as explained later in this chapter.

Release fear-based thoughts, with statements in between, "Even though," and "I can still deeply and profoundly love, forgive and accept myself." Examples: **I'm afraid what I want is never going to happen; I doubt if I'll get what I want; I don't have faith that...** (you fill in).

Affirm faith by tapping as you install, **"I have faith; I have faith that... I trust that..."** (you fill in).

Image what you want and **imagine and "experience"** how you would *feel* if you already had the faith you are creating.

If you've had many disappointments and have difficulty 'believing', program yourself for confidence and belief also.

Though they all mean the same thing, they may be recorded differently in your mind and nervous system.

Increase your **knowledge**. When you know and understand how the spiritual and mental laws operate, your faith cannot be shaken, any more than your faith in two other great laws — the laws of gravity and electricity — can be shaken. **Take action** related to your goals. By taking the action steps, you demonstrate your faith…to yourself and to the universe.

Read other people's stories of how they overcame their challenges. They can inspire you, especially when your faith is faltering. Following is one of my favorites. It reminds us that when we have the simple faith of a child, nothing is withheld from us.

One Little Girl's Miracle

When I was a Concept-Therapy instructor, I sometimes had the pleasure of joining several teachers to present a class to children. We taught the children that they could have whatever they wanted, as long as they knew what it was, *believed* it, affirmed it, imagined it and took action.

The truth is, if we condense all the teachings on the subject of how to get what you want, *those* are the steps. Almost everything else we do is for the purpose of believing -- of *creating faith*.

Vibrational Harmony

At one of the children's classes I taught, a precocious nine year old girl (we'll call her Michelle) knew exactly what she wanted, but wouldn't tell her mother. She promised to tell her when it happened. (Notice, she didn't say "if".)

Here's some personal information about Michelle. She had been born with an "outie" belly button and she hated it, especially since she had two sisters who had "innies". She decided she was going to turn her belly button into an "innie". Do you think that's impossible? I certainly did, but I didn't tell Michelle. Michelle didn't tell her mother because she knew her mother would say, "That's impossible to do, so pick something else to change." (A good lesson – don't share your dreams with someone who may tell you it's impossible!)

Four weeks after the class, Michelle, wearing a two-piece bathing suit with the bottom revealing her navel, walked into the yard where her mother and grandmother were sitting. As she approached them, she excitedly shouted: "LOOK!" They both stared in stunned silence, mouths and eyes wide open. *Michelle had an "innie" belly button!*

When asked "how" she accomplished this miracle, she explained: "Like we were taught. Every morning and night, and whenever I thought about it, I said, 'I have an innie belly button,' and I pictured myself with an innie belly button." While still in a state of shock, her mom asked, "But what did you DO? What was your *action*?"

"Oh, that puzzled me at first. Then I figured it out," Michelle replied, as she started making large circles on her stomach with her hand. "I rubbed my stomach and said, 'Go in, go in, go in!"

In my years as a Concept Therapy instructor and after, I heard and witnessed many amazing stories, but this remains my favorite. Not only is it a fun story, it illustrates how we can get what we want, no matter how impossible it seems…especially if we have child-like faith.

Integrating Faith

True faith is an inner *knowing*. Get together with other people of like mind to discuss the concepts and principles in this book. As your vibrations (energy fields) combine, everyone's certainty and faith grows. Be sure your conversations are focused on positives, not negatives — unless you are releasing or problem-solving. If you are doing the latter, be sure to put your attention on *finding solutions*.

Keep a journal to record all the good things that happen to you or around you each day, and read them. This can be in conjunction with, or separate from, your Gratitude Journal.

Read and listen to inspiring and motivating material. Keep yourself in a positive frame of mind. That gives you the positive vibrations that attract what you want. And as you get some of what you want, you develop more faith.

You Can't Control All Outcomes

It's important for you to understand that the nature of life is to both support and challenge you. Life is full of disappointments on the road to success. As you go for your goal, you'll have hits and misses along the way.

Babe Ruth, the "home run king", didn't hit all the balls (actually he struck out 1,330 times). Michael Jordan doesn't make every basket. Every famous actor fails to get parts they really want. Music icons put out recordings that don't go anywhere. The biggest show business producers and directors have multi-million dollar movies, Broadway productions and television shows that flop.

Top sales people don't sell every customer. R. H. Macy failed seven times before his New York super-store caught on. English novelist, John Creasey, received 753 rejection slips before he published 564 books – in 23 languages, no less. Probably the most famous "failure" of all (besides Lincoln, who supposedly failed at everything -- except the Presidency) is Edison who, when asked if he had ever been discouraged, said he found 10,000 ways a light bulb *doesn't* work!

No matter what you do, you can't control all the outcomes. That's life! But if you know what you want, keep your eye on your vision and take action – with determination and persistence – you'll ultimately reach your goal, especially if you add that magic ingredient…FAITH.

Chapter 32

PHYSICAL THINGS *DO* MATTER

The physical matters (no pun intended) because matter is *energy* that is vibrating at a lowered frequency. Therefore, when you use physical "things" you are still using energy.

Just know that mental energy is more powerful than physical. That's why someone can have the best physical treatment, but if he or she doesn't believe it will work, it won't. The opposite is also true. People sometimes use substances (placebos) that have no intrinsic value, and they benefit from them because they strongly believe the treatment will work.

Chronically ill people often have results with energy healing and/or alternative care that seem miraculous. This is because the therapy "turns on the energy" (the life force) and allows healing to happen. However, your body is composed of physical matter and is biochemical in nature. What you put into and on it, and what you do with it, are very important to your health and well-being. While drugs are often overused and many surgeries are unnecessary, there are times when traditional medical care is life-saving. How to handle specific health challenges is something for you and your health practitioner to decide.

Chapter 33

ACHIEVING VIBRATIONAL HARMONY

I guess you know by now that the "secret" of getting the things you want in life is to achieve vibrational harmony with them. Creation takes place in *each moment*. That means that no matter how bad your childhood was, no matter how negative your programming is, no matter how many people wronged you, no matter how many times you failed before -- you can begin creating anew, *now*, by raising your vibrations.

Positive prayer and meditation raise your vibrations. When you vibrate at a high enough frequency, your consciousness merges with the Source and you have access to all the power in the universe. If you ask for what you want from *that* state of consciousnesss, you achieve vibrational harmony with it. That's when magic and miracles happen!

The Tremendous Benefits of "Feeling Good"

Love, joy, faith, gratitude, appreciation, patience, enthusiasm, serenity – all the positive emotions – align us with our Superconscious and are in vibrational harmony with the "good" of life. Also, when you feel good, your life force flows freely, which gives you the added bonus of improved health. In contrast, emotions like anger, fear, resentment, jealousy, frustration, criticism, blame, judgment, anxiety, guilt, impatience, etc., *constrict* your life force and also put you in harmony with what we call "the bad" of life (like accidents, illness, chaos, disorder, etc.). Don't blame your negative emotions. Instead, *honor them* because they are telling you to change your thoughts and focus of attention.

The more you know about how life "works" – which is explained by the Energy Model and the laws of energy -- the more certainty and trust you have, and the more your fears, doubt and anxiety diminish. This raises your vibrations.

Being thankful and feeling appreciation are quick and easy ways to raise your vibrations. Look for things to appreciate and be grateful for, and you will receive MORE of them. Whatever you appreciate grows…in other words, it *appreciates*.

You raise your vibrations when you love, respect and take care of yourself. You raise your vibrations when you do what you love and love what you do. You raise your vibrations when you are creative – when you sing, dance, write, play an instrument, act, recite poetry, draw, paint, etc. (You don't have to be great at it – just ENJOY!) You raise your vibrations when you laugh and when you derive pleasure from other people's creativity – music, art, theater, books and other writings, etc. In short, one of the best and most reliable ways to raise your vibrations is to just *feel good*.

Everything Affects Everything

Everything – physical, mental, emotional and spiritual – vibrates. Vibrations combine and affect each other. Your vibrations are a mixture of everything about you at any given time, including your past memories, your conscious thoughts and feelings, mass mind consciousness, and, of course, your programming. In addition, your vibrations are affected by outside factors, such as the clothes you wear, colors, fragrances, foods you put into your body and the beauty (or lack of) in your surroundings. (Yes, living and/or working in clutter negatively affect your vibrations.)

Regardless of what's going on around you, however, you always have the power to change your vibrations by choosing positive thoughts, feelings and attitudes, and deciding what to give your attention to. Nothing is more powerful than your own mind. Decide to raise your vibrations by *choosing* your thoughts. Your emotions follow and *energize* those thoughts.

The Power of the Mind

In 1958, Chinese pianist, Liu Chi Kung, was considered one of the finest pianists in the world, second only to Van Cliburn. Shortly after, he was incarcerated in a Chinese prison for seven years. He emerged after that grueling experience to play the piano better than ever, only months after his release. The critics were astonished. When asked how he accomplished this remarkable feat, since he had not practiced for seven years, he said, "Every day I rehearsed all the pieces I had ever played, note by note, *in my mind.*"

Liu did not allow anything on the outside to affect his vision on the inside. That's an important lesson for all of us, for whatever is going on in a person's mind has the most influence on his or her vibrations and life.

People can be surrounded by magnificence and vibrate at a low frequency because they have a *habit of unhappiness*. These people do not respond well even to outside stimuli that others find so pleasing, like humor, nature, music, beauty, etc. Their mind is in such a negative state that they are not influenced by the positive vibrations around them. (While this is 'bad', the opposite – not being influenced by negative vibrations around you — is 'good'.)

If you have a habit of unhappiness, use the processes in this book to program happiness into your consciousness, just as you would program faith or any other trait or attribute.

What *Not* To Do

It's essential to understand that while you create *your* universe, you do not create *the* universe. Therefore, as you work on yourself, the universe still "does its thing". This means you will not always have things happen to your liking, no matter how good your attitude is, what you do (or don't do), and how positive your vibrations are.

When you first learn that you create with vibrations and your life is the result of vibrational harmony, you might make the same mistake I made – blame, criticize and condemn yourself for everything in your life that you don't like and don't want. It's easy to do this because we're taught that we "create" our lives, but we're not taught the laws that explain "how" we do this. The fact is, vibrational harmony is not just about YOU. Everything and everyone in the universe is connected.

The Laws of Polarity and Rhythm always operate, as do the agendas of other people. In addition, our energy field is affected by mass mind consciousness (the collective unconscious) and the tremendous amount of "vibrational interference" in today's high tech world. These include computers, the internet, cell phones, microwaves, power lines and television and other sense-stimulating entertainment.

This relatively new vibrational interference is on top of the massive amount of sights, smells, sounds, written material and media blasts that assail us. Our senses and nervous system are constantly being bombarded with vibrations we do not choose. This is a major reason for *strengthening* your energy field by releasing the "stuck" energy of negative programs and emotional traumas from your body, and by being conscious and aware as you continue on your life's journey.

Wisdom is essential. As the Serenity Prayer says: *"God grant me the serenity to accept what cannot be changed, the courage to change what can, and the wisdom to know the difference".*

You Don't Always "Create" It

Your company can go out of business and you may lose your job, and you didn't create it. It could rain on the day of your picnic, and you didn't create it. Merchandise might be left out of your order, and you didn't create it. An incompetent clerk can make errors, and you didn't create it. You could be caught in traffic for hours and be late for an important meeting, and you didn't create it. *It's important not to blame yourself.* It is especially important not to blame yourself if you get sick. You want to use all your energy for thinking, feeling, affirming, imaging and doing whatever is desirable and necessary to regain your health and maintain it in the future.

Now, if you *consistently* attract negative events or experiences, you need to ask *why*. Ask your Superconscious to show you what beliefs and programs in your subconscious cause you to attract what you don't want. Then ask, "How can I reprogram myself so I no longer have that program or belief?"

Identifying and releasing programs and beliefs is an on-going process. I do it all the time and teach my clients to do the same. When negative thoughts and feelings come up in the moment, I acknowledge them; then I release them. When buried beliefs and programs surface, I reprogram them. At times, I may just do something to change my mood with music, humor, prayer or meditation or by concentrating on something I love, like writing, and I do processes later.

Some illnesses and traumas are related to personal growth, for our evolutionary journey takes us through situations and events that are painful at the time – and yet, turn out to be blessings. It is important to keep your perspective and know the universe is lawful. If you blame yourself or others, rather than use your free will to *choose* your response, you lower your vibrations by holding onto negative thoughts and feelings.

Taking Care of Your Physical Body

Since everything you put in or on your body (and everything you do) vibrates and combines with your vibrations, there are physical things you can use to raise your vibrations. Drink *pure* water (at least 8 glasses a day for most adults), eat organic food, take whole food supplements and digestive enzymes (digestion uses up a great deal of your body's energy). Have an exercise program, and consider including yoga and/or tai chi. Also, release low vibrations caused by continual stress by taking a short break every 90-120 minutes (5 minutes will do) to rest or relax – even if you don't think you need to.

In addition, you can raise your vibrations by using pure essential oils and by wearing something with a computer chip to protect yourself from ELF (extra low frequency) radiation, which is incompatible with human energy fields. This includes microwaves, TV, power lines, computers, cell phones, etc. Though your state of mind is the most important, the physical does "matter". Check my website's Health section, which includes recommended products.

Chapter 34

REMEMBER THESE POINTS...

I can't tell you, in one book, everything it took me thirty years and many thousands of dollars to learn. But I can tell you this -- I wish there had been a simple book that explained the natural laws and principles behind change, growth, success and healing as this book does, when I was studying years ago. My life would have been much easier.

But then again, maybe it wasn't supposed to be easier. Maybe I had to go through what I went through – two divorces, business failures, bankruptcy, foreclosure and a life-threatening illness – so I could change my life and share this material in a way that would help others. Perhaps this is my mission. I believe it is, for nothing gives me greater pleasure than sharing what I know. I've done that in this book, and now I'll summarize the main points.

***Everything* is energy.** Though we've accepted the Material Model as "the truth", science confirms it is NOT the truth. The **Energy Model** and the universal (spiritual) and mental laws show us how life really works. You are energy and everything about you is energy. The quality of your life depends on how you use your energy (especially mental energy) to interact with the Infinite energy of the universe.

The Laws of Polarity and Rhythm are *facts of life*. This means there will always be the two sides to life – what we classify as "good" or desirable, and "bad" or undesirable. *Everyone's* life consists of pleasure and pain, support and challenge, blessings and disappointments. This is true for the rich and poor, smart and dumb, beautiful and plain. The polarities and rhythmic swings always exist on planet earth.

Your *perception* of "what is", and how much you evolve in consciousness, determines the *degree* of swings in your life. By being grateful for your blessings, letting go of what you can't control and having faith that the universe IS your friend, joy and peace will become your companions, instead of suffering and struggle. *Accept* these natural laws as reality, re-read and *use* what you learn in this book…and *focus* on what you want.

You get what you're in *vibrational harmony* with. Unless *you* choose your focus of attention, your *programs* determine what you're in vibrational harmony with. By making conscious choices that differ from your automatic responses, you change your vibrations. Many people attract what they don't want because they don't focus on what they *do* want.

Creation occurs in *each moment* -- with every thought you think, feeling you feel, word you speak and action you take, for they all vibrate into the unified energy field. Since programming determines most people's vibrations, their subconscious — not their conscious free will -- determines their life. But it doesn't have to determine *yours*.

You are *always* creating. Use the free will of your conscious mind to *deliberately* think about, image and affirm what you want, regardless of outer experiences.

***Reprogram* your subconscious mind.** Your subconscious is the computer that carries the instructions for your life. If you don't like the instructions, *you* must change them. Most people unconsciously accept negative mass mind beliefs, (especially about health, wealth and success). Through reprogramming, you can release your negative beliefs and programs, whether inherited, environmental or coming from mass mind…and reprogram yourself with *new* instructions.

Use tapping processes and breathing to *release negatives*. You can tap on anything that bothers you. You don't always change "what is" (though often you do), but you DO change your response to it. Sometimes just releasing the emotional charge is all you need in order to move on.

Call on your Superconscious* to assist you.** It's your connection to the spiritual realm (God, Guides, Angels, Higher Self, etc.), and is always ready and willing to help you. Align yourself with its high frequencies and then…ask***.

Until we meet again…may you be in vibrational harmony with your heart's desires and *get what you want!*

An Open Letter from my Heart to my Readers:

I am truly grateful that you chose to read this book. It is the culmination of many years of study, introspection and personal application.

I believe that understanding the new paradigm, the Energy Model -- including the spiritual and mental laws, the body-mind energy connection, how to manage our "computer" (the subconscious) and change our computer's operating system – is vital for living the life we want. This knowledge is especially essential in today's world, when we must be able to create order out of chaos.

My goal and purpose is to reach as many people as possible, and introduce them to this new paradigm and the concept of vibrational harmony. I know I can't do it alone. I need assistance from those who feel this knowledge and understanding is important for the public to have. One way to get the material out is to tell others about this book. Another way is to refer me to people you know, who have contacts and/or the ability to help me reach the public – through lectures, trainings, books, TV, radio, magazines or any other means.

If you belong to organizations or associations that hire speakers, please introduce me to the meeting planners. My website has wonderful testimonials about my speaking. Since I'm also a professional singer, I provide entertainment at conferences and conventions, as well as present a unique and powerful message.

If you're a health professional, who uses energy-based techniques or modalities (rather than drugs and surgery), bringing me to your area can be a powerful marketing strategy for you. I'm referring to chiropractors, acupuncturists, hypnotherapists, naturopaths, homeopaths, massage therapists, reflexologists, energy healers, energy psychologists, etc. You can host me yourself, or with other health professionals.

As you know, far too many people suffer needlessly because

Vibrational Harmony

they don't "believe in" the benefits of natural holistic care. The main reason more of them don't beat a path to your door, even though they need your services, is because *they don't see how or why you can help them*. Once they learn about the body-mind energy connection and vibrational harmony, they will.

If you sell products to professionals or consumers that raise vibrations and increase life force (or chi or prana), hosting a seminar is also an excellent marketing strategy for you. The products I have in mind include whole food supplements, organic foods, essential oils, crystals, devices to protect against inharmonious frequencies, subliminal tapes, air and water purifiers, feng shui supplies, etc. Once they learn about energy and vibrations, the audience knows *why* they need your products. As a result, they buy. You'll be instrumental in helping more people heal, and, of course, you'll greatly increase your sales.

If you're a businessperson who wants to reduce stress and accelerate change, growth, productivity and success in your company, I'd love to train your managerial, office and/or sales staff in the Energy Model and the universal and mental laws, as they apply to business. This material is the *foundation* upon which change and success is based. When your staff knows how to use the laws, they can bring your company to a new level. Not only will you help your business immeasurably, you'll impact upon, and positively influence, countless other people.

Last -- but definitely not least -- consider hosting me in your area so I can teach this life-transforming material to your colleagues, associates, friends and family members. The more people in your life who understand how life really works, the easier *your* life is.

I hope you'll be inspired to think of ways to help me get this vital material to more people, and contact me. *Everyone has the right to know.*

With Love,

Bevrly

You Can Live Your Vision

By Beverly Nadler

You can live your vision
You can live your dream --
The source to do this
Comes from an endless stream

Of Power that makes it
Possible for you
To make your dream
And vision come true.

Is there a song in your soul
You are longing to sing?
Is there a gift in your heart
You are longing to bring?

Is there something that calls you
And says follow me?
Is there an image you hold
Only you can see?

Whatever your vision
Hold it in your mind's eye --
Give it wings
Watch it fly.

You can live your vision,
Turn it into reality --
This is your Divine gift,
This is your destiny!

Copyright Beverly Nadler 2000

Would you like to see and hear Beverly in person?
Would you like her to share her message with others?
Bring Beverly to your area to teach

VIBRATIONAL HARMONY
"The Missing Link" to Getting What You Want!

A life-changing one or two day program for people who want to know how life *really* works

- DISCOVER how the universal and mental laws operate, and how your amazing mind functions
- LEARN how to reprogram your subconscious
- ENJOY more success, health, prosperity, love and confidence…whatever *you* want
- REDUCE your levels of stress and tension
- RESTORE order out of chaos
- MASTER powerful new techniques to achieve vibrational harmony – "the missing link"

… and much more

"Beverly Nadler can explain the Universal Laws of Success so simply even a child can understand them. Latch on to this lady…for she is a treasure of transformation."
Dr. Larry Markson, CEO, The Masters Circle, Inc., NY

"Astonishing in its simplicity. Thank you for putting together so much information in one place. Allows us to really see and understand the Unity of science and theology."
Rev. Linda A. Bardes, Religious Science Minister, CT

Beverly also presents training programs for businesses

Want to know how you can host Beverly?
call or email: 203-973-0130
beverlynadler@mindspring.com
www.beverlynadler.com

Tell your Meeting Planner
about Beverly for your next Conference, Convention or Special Event

"All of the attendees benefited and left with the knowledge that they had the power to change their lives."
Jacqueline Carbe, Senior Meeting Planner, AIPLA, VA.

"One of our most memorable and appreciated speakers. Your clarity, presence and style added to the undersanding and enjoyment of the fascinating material.
Michael Ringel, CCO, Let's Talk Business Network, Inc., NY

A motivating and dynamic speaker, as well as an acclaimed singer and performer, Beverly gives an awesome presentation that is as entertaining and enjoyable as it is enlightening and inspiring.

You can be the catalyst that brings a new and different program to your Organization, Association, Company or Group -- one that will open their minds and touch their hearts. Beverly's beautiful voice enhances her brilliant presentation as she shares some of the profound principles in her book. An unforgettable experience!

Beverly also teaches 1 – 3 hour seminars and workshops at Conferences, Conventions and Business and Sales meetings

Want to know more?

call or email: 203-973-0130
beverlynadler@mindspring.com
www.beverlynadler.com

RESOURCES

BEVERLY'S BOOKS AND TAPES

Dynamic Self-Healing Manuals - $135

This is a simplified, correlated integration of ancient wisdom and modern science that explains and clarifies the universal and mental laws that govern our lives. The manuals take the confusion out of self-help and personal growth. They also provide a great deal of information on stress management, nutrition, and alternative and holistic healing therapies and products.

"These are not really books, but home study courses that synthesize years and years of study, training and personal experience. Our blessed author was born to write these books."
Joseph Polansky, Sarasota, FL

How to Get What You Want (Secrets of Success, Health and Money) $15 (co-authored)

A delightful book full of wisdom, wit and meaningful "thoughts on a page". It will inspire you, motivate you and give you ideas to meditate upon.

"Without question, this is the best of the daily thought books I have ever read, and I've read many." Mac Stern, Stamford, CT

Success Through Self-Confidence Audio Tape $12

An audiotape that explains how the mind works and how to develop self-confidence. It's full of practical, valuable easy-to-do techniques that really work.

"Thank you for the enormous changes I have been able to make in my life. I was very depressed, didn't care much about anything. Your tape gave me so many wonderful things to do. And they work! Thank you." Linda Westly, San Diego, CA

To order Beverly's materials, contact:

Unlimited Visions
911 East Main Street (Suite #249)
Stamford, Connecticut 06902

203-973-0130

email: <u>beverlynadler@mindspring.com</u>

website addresses: <u>www.beverlynadler.com</u> or <u>www.youcanliveyourvision.com/beverly</u>

Check the website periodically for new articles, past issues of newsletter and recommended new health products.

SCWL SUBLIMINAL TAPES - $29.95
(order 2 and receive the 3rd FREE)

Over 130 titles. *New: 20 CDs and more coming*
Tapes are sold with a money back guarantee

"I am amazed at the changes that have taken place in such a short time after I began using SCWL tapes. I am much more confident, my memory has improved, I feel better about life in general and – miracle of miracles – I'm losing weight. Thank you so much." Shellie Cohen, New York, NY

For information on SCWL tapes, including titles and testimonials, check the website. If you do not have internet access, contact Beverly.

BEVERLY'S SERVICES

- Keynotes for Conferences, Conventions, Events
- Seminars (see * next page)
- Business and Sales Trainings
- Programs you host in your area

- Coaching - Personal telephone coaching
- Business and Professional Consulting and Coaching
- Complimentary 10 minute telephone consultation

*Seminar topics include: Personal Growth, Stress Mastery, Holistic Health, Stop Smoking, Business and Professional Success, Building Order Out of Chaos, Communication Skills, Relationships…and more

All programs customized for clients

For more information, check website and contact Beverly at Unlimited Visions.

To be on Beverly's personal mailing list, send name, address, phone and e-mail address to
beverlynadler@mindspring.com

To subscribe to Beverly's **"Live Your Vision" newsletter** send e-mail to above address with "subscribe" in subject line OR send a blank e-mail to:
liveyourvisionnewsletter-subscribe@topica.com

RECOMMENDED BOOKS

There are many excellent books on personal and spiritual growth, with new ones coming out all the time. The only ones on this list are about energy and universal law, reprogramming the subconscious mind or using energy psychology techniques.

- **Getting Through to Your Emotions With EFT --** Phillip and Jane Mountrose
- **Extraordinary Healing** -- Marilyn Gordon
- **Stepping Free of Limiting Patterns With Essence Repatterning** – Pat McCallum

- **Feelings Buried Alive Never Die** – Karol K. Truman
- **Freedom From Fear Forever** – Dr. James V. Durlacher
- **Count Your Blessings** – Dr. John Demartini
- **The Holographic Universe** (Quantum Physics) -- Michael Talbot
- **The Kybalion** (Hermetic Philosophy) – Three Initiates
- **Rays of the Dawn** – Dr. Thurman Fleet

If your bookstore does not have these books, they should be able to order them, or try **www.amazon.com**

TRAININGS THAT TEACH UNIVERSAL LAW

- **Concept-Therapy Institute:** 800-531-5628
- **Silva Mind Method:** 800-545-MIND
- **Silva Mind Method of New York:**
  Tony Mitchell - 212-698-0123
- **Dr. John Demartini's "Breakthrough":**
  contact Dr. Denise Nadler, 203-969-2829
- **Kaballah:** The ancient mystical Jewish teachings are about universal law. Though Kaballah is a complex and intense study, there are some books and courses for laypeople. Check your bookstore, local adult education programs and classes by independent lecturers.

See next page for Order Form to order Beverly's materials.

Vibrational Harmony

ORDER FORM

Two Dynamic Self-Healing Manuals (*DSH) $135
  Ship/hndl $10 (Canada – $15)

How to Get What You Want (*HGWW) $15
Success Thru Self-Confidence (*STSC) $12
Vibrational Harmony   (*VH) $22

(US shipping/handling -- $4.50 first item. Add
    $1.50, 2nd and 3rd item, $1.00 additional items)
(email or call for int'l shipping and quantity discounts)

*Use initials to designate products you are ordering

Product _____ Qnty @_____Cost_____
Product _____ Qnty @_____Cost_____
Product _____ Qnty @_____Cost_____

                         Shp/hndlng_____

                         Total_____
Method of Payment   _____Check   _____Money Order
    _____Amex/MC/Visa

Name_____

Address_____

City_____State_____Zip_____

Telephone_____

E-mail_____

CREDIT CARD# _____
EXP:_____
NOTE: Charge is from DREAMSPLASH

The Elven Brooch™

An exact reproduction of the leaf brooch worn by the members of the Fellowship of the Ring from

ABOUT BEVERLY

Beverly Nadler is a dynamic speaker, trainer, consultant, reprogramming coach and award-winning author. At conventions, conferences and special events, she offers unique programs that are as entertaining as they are enlightening. In coaching and training, she works with individuals and companies on issues related to personal development, self-esteem, health, stress management, professional success and team building.

A popular media guest who appeared on *"Good Morning, New York"*, Beverly is a certified hypnotherapist and member of the *International Association of Counselors and Therapists*. In addition to speaking and writing, her background includes sales and marketing, managing a natural health care facility and owning and operating a Stop Smoking Center in New York.

Native New Yorker, now living in CT, Beverly is also a published poet and professional cabaret and theatre singer who has three daughters and one granddaughter. She speaks nationally and in Canada (and welcomes invitations from other countries) and frequently teaches at the Learning Annex in NYC.

Beverly's teaching correlates and integrates the ancient wisdom of metaphysics and Hermetic Philosophy with the scientific breakthroughs of psychology and modern physics. The turning point in Beverly's life came in 1993-94, when she used everything she knew to recover from a critical illness. In the process of healing her body, she healed her life. Today, her teaching comes out of her own life-transforming experience, as well as her years of research, study and working with others.

Beverly's mission is to help people get more of what they want out of life. She does this by sharing little-known, essential information and teaching a dynamic new technology for change.

ISBN 1552128547